TRIUMPH TR

From Beginning to End

OTHER TITLES IN THE CROWOOD AUTOCLASSICS SERIES

TRIUMPH TR

From Beginning to End

Kevin Warrington

For Michael
with Best Wishes

Kevin Warrington.

THE CROWOOD PRESS

First published in 2016 by

The Crowood Press Ltd

Ramsbury, Marlborough

Wiltshire SN8 2HR

www.crowood.com

British Library Cataloguing-in-Publication Data

A catalogue record for this book is available from the British Library.

ISBN 978 1 78500 187 1

Typeset and designed by D & N Publishing, Baydon, Wiltshire

Printed and bound in India by Parksons Graphics

CONTENTS

ACKNOWLEDGEMENTS

The images acknowledged with the BMIHT credit are from the British Motor Industry Heritage Trust. These are © BMIHT. All publicity material and photographs originally produced for/by the British Leyland Motor Corporation, British Leyland Ltd and Rover Group, including all its subsidiary companies, are the copyright of the British Motor Industry Heritage Trust and reproduced here with their permission. Permission to use images does not imply the assignment of copyright, and anyone wishing to re-use this material should contact BMIHT for permission to do so.

There are so many people to thank for their support and assistance in writing this book and creating the photographs. The following books are amongst those consulted to confirm much of the detail and are recommended as further reading on the subject:

Triumph Cars – The Complete Story, Robson, Graham and Langworth, Richard (MRP Publishing Ltd, 1988)
Triumph TRs – The Complete Story, Robson, Graham (Crowood, 1991)
Triumph TR, Piggott, Bill (Haynes Publishing, 2003)
Triumph TR7: The Untold Story, Knowles, David (Crowood, 2007)
The Works Triumphs, Robson, Graham (Foulis & Co., 1993)
Works Triumphs in Detail, Robson, Graham (Herridge & Sons, 2014)

Members of the local Triumph clubs in Hampshire, Berkshire and Dorset were unfailing in their help and support, especially in helping me to locate cars to photograph, particularly thanks to the TR Register and TR Drivers' Club. Having found the cars, I must acknowledge my thanks to all the owners who indulged my desire to photograph their vehicles. In particular, I would like to highlight Michael Eatough and Steve Harridge (TR2), Ben Wood and David Erskine (TR3), Phil Webb (TR3A), Nigel Jordan, Phil Bishop and Hillary Bagshaw (TR4/4A). Hillary was able to supply the same car and identify the original location to replicate the photographs used in the earlier 'Complete Story' book. Michael Field allowed me to photograph his TR5, Tony Alderton provided a couple of pictures of his TR250, the TR6 pictures are mostly of a car formerly owned by me and a second car owned by Phil Bishop, and the TR7s were provided by Phil Lines and David Reeve. The Peerless was provided by Peter Hudspath, who fortuitously arrived at an event that I was attending in a different capacity; the delightful Italia is owned by Paul Harvey and the Grinnall by Phil Horsley. Ian Cornish and Neil Revington both allowed me access to photograph their former works cars, 4 VC and 6 VC. Other pictures are from my collection; where the photograph was not taken specifically for use in this book, the vehicle registration details have been deliberately removed.

An enjoyable day was spent with Brian Culcheth who shared some of his photograph collection and reminiscences of his time as a works driver.

The background research material for the Doretti and Peerless sections was sourced from the model registers, and Adrian C. Sinnott and Paul Harvey provided extensive information for the Italia. Thank you all for your help – it really was much appreciated.

INTRODUCTION

So much has been written before on the subject of Triumph's aspirational sports cars that writing a new history brings with it various challenges, not least of which is that almost everything of historical note has been amply covered in works by authors with far greater insight than I could ever hope to possess. It is inevitable that, in writing this new book, I have drawn extensively on material that has been previously published as so much of it is established historical fact.

It is important to understand the origins of the business, so I have started the story with its foundations. Like so many businesses in the Coventry area, it began as a cycle manufacturer that went on to build motor cars; before that, it had been a manufacturer and reseller of sewing machines.

For much of its life, the Standard-Triumph company dealt with numerous difficult financial issues, the more significant of which are addressed in this book. Not least of these were the social, economic and industrial challenges that were created once Standard-Triumph found itself a part of the British Leyland empire.

Perhaps because of the need to generate cash flow, the company was willing to sell its technology to others who developed motor cars in what today might be described as 'niche' markets, based to a greater or lesser extent on Triumph TR underpinnings. Some of these cars, particularly the Michelotti-designed Italia, built by Vignale on a TR3 base, are highly sought after and financially appreciating classics, while others are less well known but just as interesting. In addition, major components, from suspension systems to engines and transmissions, have made an appearance in sports cars built by manufacturers that can only be considered as rivals to Triumph.

'Triumph by name, Triumph by nature' describes the success of the TR on both the circuit and in rallying. This book will also document some of the key milestones in Triumph's sporting success.

CHAPTER ONE

IN THE BEGINNING

The Triumph TR can be said to have been born in the austerity years following the Second World War, a product of the Standard-Triumph Company. Its essential DNA had been formed in the products of the former Triumph Company, a firm with its roots in Coventry and, like so many enterprises to have evolved from that Midlands city, having strong connections with sewing machines and bicycles. The Triumph Company quickly established a well-deserved reputation for quality motor vehicles with a sporting character to their design. Insolvency in 1939 and a short-term rescue resulted in the acquisition of the remnants of the business by the Standard Motor Company in 1945. An inspired decision of Standard was the use of the Triumph brand, initially for the sports cars and, eventually, for the entire output of the company.

If the closing years of the twentieth century and the early years of the twenty-first have been dominated by information technology and communication, the closing years of the nineteenth century and most of the twentieth were marked by a desire for personal transportation. The growth of the bicycle industry led to the formation of many businesses that were to become household names with more developed forms of transport, and much of this industry settled on the city of Coventry in the West Midlands of England. Coventry itself is an ancient settlement with origins predating the larger local cities of Birmingham and Leicester, becoming a manufacturing centre for precision engineering as early as the eighteenth century with the development of clock-making. A local skilled workforce was therefore ready for the development and manufacture of the safety bicycle, starting in 1885 with the 'Rover Safety Bicycle' and leading inexorably to the addition of an internal combustion engine to form the motorcycle. While the motor car as we know it has its origins in the design of Karl Benz's *Motorwagen* of 1885, it was the city of Coventry that was to become a significant design and manufacturing centre for the industry until quite recent times.

Born in 1863 in Nuremburg, Germany, Siegfried Bettmann moved to England in 1885, settling at first in London. With the ability to speak several languages fluently, he found employment initially with Kelly and Co., compiling foreign trade directories. Within six months, Bettmann was engaged at the London office of the White Sewing Machine Company of Cleveland, Ohio, as Representative for 'foreign countries'. Following a quarrel with George Sawyer, manager of the White Company, Bettmann set up on his own account as S. Bettmann & Company, acting as agent for a number of German-owned businesses. Identifying a growing market for the bicycle, he commissioned the William Andrews Company of Birmingham to manufacture a suitable machine that he could sell using his established contacts both at home and internationally. 'Triumph' was the brand name chosen to market the bicycles. A sea change in the future success of S. Bettmann & Company occurred in 1887 when fellow German Mauritz Schulte, also originally from Nuremburg, joined Bettmann as a partner and encouraged Bettmann to develop the company as a manufacturing business.

With Coventry already established as the centre of the bicycle manufacturing world, Bettmann's company soon relocated, finding premises in Much Park Street. Very rapidly the sewing machine interests were allowed to wain as the manufacture of cycles became the primary focus of the business, which was prospering despite the very limited capital available to it. A third former resident of Nuremberg, one Philip Schloss, was engaged to operate an office for the firm in London and he invested his life savings of £100 into the business.

With a need for a further expansion, Triumph Cycle Company Limited was incorporated as a Limited Liability Company in 1897. As well as Messrs Bettmann, Schulte and Schloss, the Directors included Alderman A.S. Tomson, owner of the Much Park Street premises and Mayor of Coventry, Alfred Friedlander, a trader and financier; George Sawyer, Bettmann's former manager at the White Sewing Machine Company, was appointed Chairman.

Business was brisk, but the Triumph cycle was a minor player in a burgeoning market. However, the interests of bicycle manufacturers and those of pneumatic tyre manufactures were closely aligned, and the business attracted the attention of Harvey du Cros of the Dunlop Company, who decided to invest significant capital into it. The connection with the Dunlop Company led to an increase in sales outlets and a significant boost to the business, such that, when shares in the company were offered to the public, the offer was more than ten times oversubscribed.

SIEGFRIED BETTMANN – THE CITIZEN

Having moved to England, Siegfried Bettmann quickly adopted his new home and once he had moved to Coventry played a full and active part in civic life. He became a Freemason and joined the local Liberal Party, standing for and being elected as a local councillor. He was also appointed as a Justice of the Peace and a founder member of the city's Chamber of Commerce. In 1913, he was appointed Mayor of Coventry, the first non-British citizen to be elected to such a post. He was a naturalized British citizen, but, as a German by birth, he was lucky to avoid internment with the changing political situation in Europe. He was forced to resign other directorships, including (ironically, as will be seen later) one with the Standard Motor Company. He resigned from his Masonic Lodge and, by November 1914, he had also resigned as Mayor. Unfounded personal attacks in the *Daily Mail* accused him of sending company profits to Germany, but he sued, won the case and was awarded damages. After the Armistice, Bettmann unveiled a memorial in 1921 to the sixty-six employees of the company who had fallen in the Great War. The memorial is located in the London Road Cemetery of Coventry.

Bettmann married a Coventry woman, Annie Meyrick (known as Millie), and founded the Annie Bettmann Foundation to assist young men and women from Coventry wishing to establish their own business, with preference given to former service men and women, or to further their education. The Foundation is still in existence.

Siegfried Bettmann died in September 1951 at his home in Stoke Park, Coventry.

Alderman Siegfried Bettmann, Mayor of Coventry 1914–15, painted in 1914 by Charles Daniel Ward.

REPRODUCED WITH THE PERMISSION OF THE HERBERT ART GALLERY AND MUSEUM, COVENTRY

THE FIRST
TRIUMPH MOTORCYCLE

It was inevitable that a successful manufacturer of bicycles would consider adding an engine to the product. Schulte, whom history records as being perhaps more forward-looking and adventurous than Bettmann, had proposed acquiring the rights to a motorcycle designed and being built in Germany by Hildebrand and Wolfmüller; Bettmann discussed the possibilities of building a motorcycle and tricycle designed by Humber but nothing resulted. Perhaps the cyclical nature of the economy had a bearing on their decisions. The middle years of the 1890s had seen the economy booming and with the inevitable slowdown following as the century drew to a close, with even the Triumph Company showing a loss on its balance sheet in 1899. It was therefore not until 1902 that Triumph was able to expand its business into motorcycles with the addition of a Minerva engine bolted into a strengthened bicycle frame and with the drive to the rear wheel. In 1905 Triumph introduced a machine incorporating its own engine design.

Competition success came early to Triumph in the Isle of Man TT races with Triumph machines taking second and third position in the 1907 single-cylinder TT, first place in the 1908

equivalent race, with four of the top five placings being achieved on Triumphs, and five of the top fifteen places in the 1909 Open Class, racing in that year against both 500cc and 750cc machines. This set a pattern that was to epitomize Triumph's motorsport activity: the brand name was always to be found in the top positions even when it was not the outright winner.

In 1907 the company moved into new premises in Priory Street. The Much Park Street building was retained as home to the lower-cost bicycle brand 'Gloria' – a name that will crop up again later in the story.

The world was turned upside down in 1914 with the outbreak of war in Europe. In the commercial world, war brings winners and losers and in the case of Triumph it brought a clear advantage for the business, notwithstanding the effect that the conflict had on the individuals employed within the company. It began with a call from a staff officer at the War Office, Captain Claude Holbrook, enquiring whether Triumph could ship a consignment of motorcycles for service in France. The success of this initial shipment led to some 30,000 'Trusty Triumphs' being supplied for war work up to the end of hostilities in 1918. The relationship between Holbrook, later Colonel Sir Claude Holbrook, and Bettmann was evidently a fruitful one, with Holbrook being invited to become Works Manager at Triumph in 1919 following Mauritz Schulte's retirement.

Introduced in 1914, the Triumph Junior was a popular single-cylinder motorcycle that was to evolve rapidly into the Model H – the model of choice for the War Office.

NATIONAL MOTOR MUSEUM

SIR CLAUDE HOLBROOK MEMORIES

Lt-Col Sir Claude Holbrook talked about the development of the Triumph Company in a recorded interview that today forms part of the Archive of the University of Coventry. The entire interview may be found within the Coventry University CURVE/open collection, curve.coventry.ac.uk. These extracts are reproduced with the kind permission of the university.

The interview begins with Holbrook describing his position at the War Office and his involvement in the introduction of mechanical transport to the Army. With the outbreak of the First World War in August 1914 the Triumph Model H was selected as the primary motorcycle for the Army:

> It was a simply designed machine, 500cc, belt drive, no gearbox and a very simple front spring form. I personally was well-acquainted with the model. I had owned myself three between 1910 and 1914 and had found it to be a well-made and very reliable machine.
>
> It must have been about August 6th 1914 that I was authorised to phone Mr Bettmann in Coventry. He told me that he had about fifty machines in stock and I told him to dispatch them that day to an Army depot in Bulford.

Holbrook was authorized to procure the entire output of Triumph motorcycles, but even this was insufficient to meet the growing need for transport and additional machines were obtained.

It was evident that dispatch riders and others always tried to get allotted a Triumph and undoubtedly the Triumph H was the popular machine with the Army.

Sir Claude first encountered Bettmann shortly after the outbreak of hostilities during a meeting at the War Office. It was the beginning of both a business association and a personal friendship. In 1917, the War Office Mechanical Transport Department was transferred to the Ministry of Munitions, with Holbrook's position as Assistant also transferring. Later in the same year, Holbrook was promoted to head the Department prior to his resignation from the Army towards the end of 1919:

> Mr Bettmann came to see me and said that now I was no longer in the Army he felt free to speak to me and invited me to join the board of Triumph Company as Works Director. I accepted and went to Coventry late November 1919.

Holbrook remembered the 1920s as a period of 'boom and bust' in the motorcycle industry:

> Competition got more intense and the motorcycle did not appear to be a lasting business. This was the moment when Triumph tried to enter the car business, but with meagre success... The motorcycle business was sold in spite of signs of recovery, the car business was too competitive and the Triumph factory was not designed for mass production and just before the Second World War the same thing happened to Triumph as to many more car firms before and since.

At an unidentified location, a group of Army dispatch riders pose on their 'Trusty Triumphs'.
NATIONAL MOTOR MUSEUM

TRIUMPH ENTERS THE CAR BUSINESS

Claude Holbrook had clear ideas about moving the company into the production of motor cars. With the war over, the economy apparently set for a buoyant period and a large potential market of recently de-mobbed servicemen, the market looked promising. The same view was taken by a significant number of other businesses, which eagerly entered the club of motor car manufacturers. Within ten years, however, most had either failed or had been absorbed into other groups. With Triumph's acquisition in 1921 of the Dawson Car Company, another Coventry-based business that had designed and were building a 'light car' of 12HP, its entrée into the motor-car business was achieved. Along with that business came additional premises at Clay Lane, located at the edge of the city in the area of Stoke.

April 1923 saw the introduction of the first Triumph car, designated the model 10/20. The first number represented the RAC horsepower, a figure used purely for tax-raising purposes, while the second indicated the actual brake horse-power developed by the engine. A number of quite orthodox designs of generally increasing power followed up to 1927, when Triumph announced a small car, the 'Super Seven'. It was very much in keeping with the famous Austin Seven and similar in many respects, except that the Triumph was more expensive, justified perhaps by the higher standard of finish. Setting a mark for the future, one of the model types available was a two-seat open coupé with an occasional 'dickey seat', a car with sporting pretensions and described by its makers as a car for 'the man who motors for the sake of motoring'.

A well-preserved example of Triumph's answer to the market's requirement for a quality car in the 7HP range – the Super Seven – seen here arriving at an event held to commemorate, among other anniversaries, ninety years since the first Triumph car was produced.

Five years later, the Super Seven was renamed as the 'Super Eight', again the model number representing the fiscal horsepower. Sporting success for Triumph cars came to match that achieved by the motorcycles, although this was the work of enthusiastic owners without factory support at this stage. In 1929 Donald Healey entered a Super Seven in the Monte-Carlo Rally. After driving through formidable weather, he arrived outside of the designated time, but he had more success the following year when he finished in seventh place overall. In 1931, Healey was the winner, this time driving an Invicta, and two years later he joined Triumph as Experimental Manager.

A NICHE MARKET

Since the company lacked the production facilities to compete with the likes of Austin and Morris, a decision to concentrate the production on a more refined and upmarket model was inevitable if the business was to prosper. A succession of distinctive designs emerged during the 1930s, showing the skill and artistry of Walter Belgrove, a name that has a particular importance in the story of the TR. Donald Healey had been influenced by the Alfa-Romeo 8C, and a small number of open sports cars fitted with inline 8-cylin-

der engines were built and given the name 'Dolomite'. Healey entered one in the 1935 Monte-Carlo Rally but retired after an accident with a train in Denmark.

An extensive range of 4- and 6-cylinder engine models were built up to 1938, a combination of saloon and open cars, the majority fitted with engines designed by Coventry-Climax and built by Triumph; the cars were given the model designation of 'Gloria', a name that had previously been used within the bicycle business.

Perhaps the most characteristic of all pre-war Triumph models were the original Dolomites, built from 1936 onwards. These were powered by Triumph's own 4- or 6-cylinder ohv engines and featured traditional saloon bodies alongside two-door coupés. One eye-catching feature of these cars was the radiator grille, frequently described as a 'waterfall' grille and a design totally in keeping with the Art Deco and streamlining design motifs of the time.

For those who found the look of the grille a little too avant-garde for their taste, Triumph also offered the Vitesse model, which was similar, but fitted with a more traditional-looking grille. Shortly before the outbreak of the Second World War, a much more conventional-looking Model Twelve was introduced, but the outbreak of hostilities severely limited its success in the market.

A Classic racing event at the Silverstone circuit: of the three Dolomite 8C cars built, at least one still survives and continues to be used in 2015 as its designers intended.

Setting a style for cutaway doors that was to return some twenty years later, this Triumph Gloria from the early 1930s reflects Triumph's pre-war engineering and style at their peak.

Totally in keeping with the Art Deco movement of the time, the design of 1930s radiators was anything but subtle.

RIGHT: **For customers who found the Dolomite radiator style too startling, a more conventional design was also offered.**

BELOW: **The 1930s Dolomite tourer was a stylish design that set out the elements of the Triumph Roadster to follow some years later.**

FINANCIAL DIFFICULTIES

Despite continued expansion, Triumph's limited production facilities meant that the firm was not in a position to manufacture in the quantities of, for example, Austin or Morris. However, they were faring better than the thirty or so other car manufacturers that had entered the market in the early 1920s and had failed to weather the storm of the Depression years of the 1930s. Disposals started in 1932 with the sale of the bicycle business and the motorcycle business was sold in 1936 to Jack Sangster, owner of Ariel. Siegfried Bettmann retired from the company in 1933, having promoted Claude Holbrook to the position of Assistant Managing Director and appointing a new Chairman in Lord Leigh, who had experience in the motor trade in connection with Armstrong-Siddeley. Holbrook succeeded

Bettmann as MD later in 1933. Profits were falling and shareholders had not received a dividend since 1930, but the decision was still taken to open a new factory at Holbrook Lane in 1935. With car production now focused on the new facility, all motorcycle production was located in the city, making for a tidy disposal to its new owner, under whose tenure it was to prosper. Despite meagre profits at the car business, investment in the new models was significant and the company was soon in serious financial difficulty. Initially, part of the new factory at Holbrook Lane became involved with aircraft-engine manufacturing as part of the build-up to the anticipated war, but, with more than £150,000 owed to the bank, the receivers were called in. With the assistance of Donald Healey, they sold the business as a going concern to Thomas W. Ward & Company.

ABOVE AND OPPOSITE PAGE TOP: **Described in the Triumph catalogue as 'The Car that is Different', the Gloria 'Free Flow' was a glamorous design with distinct tones of a Bentley. It was produced in very limited numbers.**

STANDARD TO THE RESCUE

Throughout the hostilities, the Triumph buildings were put to work in support of the war effort, but they did suffer damage as a result of the bombing raids on Coventry. Thomas Ward showed little interest in motor-car assembly and the stark reality was that the works were in ruins and the machine tools had suffered a similar fate. What had not been destroyed had been sold off. The true value of the business lay in the name; Ward's were not prepared to support the plans of Donald Healey to continue car building and this led to his departure. The value of the rump business would be with another car company and the search to find a suitable home for the Triumph marque began. Austin, Nuffield Group, Ford and Vauxhall had no need of the Triumph intellectual property, while Rootes

Group, also located in Coventry, already comprised a number of discrete brands, each with its own characteristics and with the Sunbeam and Talbot brands already overlapping with Triumph. This left the Standard Motor Company where, coincidentally, Siegfried Bettmann had taken the office of Chairman for a short period just prior to the Great War. Standard's General Manager, Captain (later Sir) John Black, had visionary plans to expand his business and the acquisition of the Triumph name gave him an opportunity to do so.

The Standard Motor Company had been established in Coventry in 1903 by Reginald Maudslay, formerly a civil engineer and a close relative to the Maudslay family that was well known in the world of commercial vehicles. In the early 1920s, Standard were a significant market player, the name reflecting its dictionary definition, but, in common with Triumph, by the

SIR JOHN BLACK

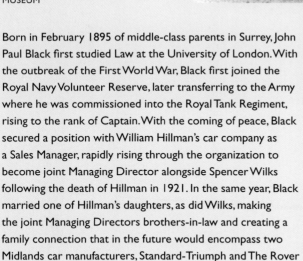

Sir John Black poses on one of the early post-war Standard products, the Phase I Vanguard; it fully met the government's mandate of 'export or die' by selling in large numbers overseas.
© BMIHT VIA NATIONAL MOTOR MUSEUM

Born in February 1895 of middle-class parents in Surrey, John Paul Black first studied Law at the University of London. With the outbreak of the First World War, Black first joined the Royal Navy Volunteer Reserve, later transferring to the Army where he was commissioned into the Royal Tank Regiment, rising to the rank of Captain. With the coming of peace, Black secured a position with William Hillman's car company as a Sales Manager, rapidly rising through the organization to become joint Managing Director alongside Spencer Wilks following the death of Hillman in 1921. In the same year, Black married one of Hillman's daughters, as did Wilks, making the joint Managing Directors brothers-in-law and creating a family connection that in the future would encompass two Midlands car manufacturers, Standard-Triumph and The Rover Company.

In 1928, Black was also appointed to the boards of Humber and Commer, which would be brought together formally the following year with their absorption into the Rootes Group. Both Wilkes and Black found their position within the new Rootes organization difficult and joined rival companies, Wilks going to Rover and Black joining the Standard Motor Company, becoming Managing Director in 1933. With war

looming in the late 1930s, Black fully supported the Government's policy of constructing 'shadow factories', constructing and operating two that would with the coming of peace become part of the manufacturing facility for Standard. He was knighted in 1943 in recognition of his work with the wartime Aero Engine Committee, arranged the acquisition of the Triumph concern in 1945 and rose to the position of Chairman of the new organization in 1953.

John Black had a reputation among his workforce for being abrasive and dictatorial and that attitude extended to his fellow directors. Towards the end of 1953, Ken Richardson was demonstrating the new Swallow Doretti to Sir John, who was being transported in the car as a passenger when an accident occurred, causing injuries to Black. The official line was that Black retired shortly after due to declining health, but it is true to say that the board had already had grave concerns regarding an agreement with Ferguson and Black's plans to dismiss his deputy.

Sir John Black died in December 1965. Quoting his successor, Alick Dick, *Autocar* described Black in an article published in October 1971 as an 'extrovert and exciting, if somewhat controversial personality'.

later 1920s they were experiencing difficult financial issues. At this point, Captain Black, who had established a reputation within the Coventry car-manufacturing circles for having well-developed organizational skills and an ability to make things happen, joined from Hillman. Black had close family connections with local businesses; his father-in-law was William Hillman and Spencer Wilks of Rover was his brother-in-law. Black transformed the fortunes of Standard such that it came to be considered among the 'big six' British car manufacturers.

In addition to building their own cars, Standard also sold major components to other businesses operating in specific markets, including what was then the Swallow Sidecar Company and later became SS-Jaguar and eventually Jaguar.

The addition of a brand with a sporting heritage was clearly attractive – not that the Standard product range was particularly staid. In an era when many volume production cars featured very similar four-light and six-light bodies, Standard cars were easily identified, with the 'Flying' model cars being particularly attractive.

The merger of the two companies was completed in April 1945, with Sir John Black being appointed Chairman and Managing Director of Triumph Motor Company (1945) Ltd, a wholly owned subsidiary of the Standard Motor Company Ltd. With the coming of peace in 1945, Triumph had been rescued and its name was about to reappear, but now on cars with Standard underpinnings.

With many British car designs of the 1930s and early post-war years looking very similar, Standard's 'Flying' models were distinctively stylish.

CHAPTER TWO

THE BIRTH OF THE TR

The Triumph brand is reborn with the Renown and the Roadster, based on pre-war Standard components. Standard also introduce the Vanguard, with a new engine that finds use in applications as widespread as agricultural tractors and rally-winning sports cars. The Triumph sports car begins to evolve, with the TR-X and 20TS being early designs before the familiar and highly successful TR2 appears, in 1953.

When production of motor cars for the civilian market recommenced after the end of the war, there had of course been little or no development since 1939 and it was quite obvious that the models first on the market would be those last sold prior to the hostilities. In the case of Standard, this meant the 'Flying' models. The race was on to introduce new, post-war products, taking advantage of the skills learned by most car manufacturers who had been engaged in the war effort for six years. In the case of Standard-Triumph, the first new models were to be badged as Triumphs, but would share nothing mechanical with the pre-war models. The chassis were constructed from tubular steel, shortened in the case of the Roadster, as a result of strict rationing of steel sheet, and the running gear was substantially the same as that used in the Standard 14. In both cases, the 1776cc overhead-valve engine was a 4-cylinder unit of the same type supplied to Jaguar.

The generic 'Renown' saloon car revitalized the 'razor-edge' styling popular on coachbuilt cars and was said to fulfil Sir John Black's ideas of an upmarket small limousine.

In fact, Standard had also been supplying a 6-cylinder engine of similar design to Jaguar and Sir John Black had ambitions to challenge Sir William Lyons' company. Where the two models differed was the body style. The saloon featured a distinctive 'razor-edge' styling of the type made popular in the late 1930s on coachbuilt limousines designed by Mulliners of Birmingham to a general specification by Sir John Black. It could have been seen as somewhat dated by

1945. Marketed variously as Triumph 1800, Triumph 2000 and Triumph Renown, the models are today frequently referred to generically as 'Renowns'.

The Roadster was a throwback to the 1930s, seating three across in the front with a column gear change and a dickey seat for occasional passengers. The dickey-seat passengers were provided with a rudimentary windscreen but no weather equipment. A young and talented designer by

Enjoying popularity once again in the 1980s as a result of 'starring' in a TV series set on the island of Jersey, the Triumph Roadster was the first new Triumph to be announced from the reborn company.

HOW THINGS COULD HAVE BEEN: CECIL KIMBER

What place can Cecil Kimber, the famous General Manager of MG, have in a book about Triumph cars? Kimber's relationship with Morris began in 1921 when he was appointed as Sales Manager of Morris Garages. In 1922, after the apparent suicide of Edward Armstead, General Manager of the business, Kimber found himself promoted and filling that role. A talented draughtsman, he had a gift for distinctive and eye-catching designs for the run-of-the-mill Morris cars – some described them as looking as though they were travelling fast even when stationary. With tuned engines, these 'MG' cars were sold at a substantial premium but still found a ready market. By 1935, MG had been brought back into the Nuffield empire, but personality differences between Kimber, Lord Nuffield and Managing Director Leonard Lord (later Lord

Lambury) gradually became an issue. By 1944 Kimber had left the company with which his name would be for ever linked. An approach by Sir John Black to a senior position within Triumph was considered, but dismissed. Perhaps Kimber thought that the personality clash would cause the same problems as it had at MG?

Cecil Kimber had a meeting planned with diesel engine manufacturer Perkins in Peterborough on 5 February 1944. The evening before, the train on which Kimber was travelling stalled as it was passing through the tunnels at the exit of King's Cross station. The train slipped back down the gradient and collided with a signal gantry and Kimber was one of two passengers to be killed.

the name of Frank Callaby was responsible for the design, but it was Sir John who had insisted on the dickey seat; it was the last car to be built with such a feature. Overall, the car bore a similarity with the Dolomite coupés of immediate pre-war construction. Not only was the Triumph name saved, but the familiar globe trademark was also present on new vehicles again.

STANDARDIZATION AND CHANGE

Changes to the Roadster in its three-year lifetime were limited to a new engine of 2088cc capacity, an engine that in various states of tune and capacity was to be found in all models

The TR-X outside the works in Coventry. When shown at the Paris and London Motor Shows, the car provoked a mixed reaction; its lasting legacy was to set a different path for the Roadsters that were to follow.
© BMIHT

Photographed outside Charlecote Park in Warwickshire, the front three-quarter view of the TR-X shows off Walter Belgrove's styling to its greatest advantage. Just visible behind the front wheel is a small badge with the letter 'B', an indulgence granted to Belgrove to recognize his involvement in the design.
© BMIHT VIA NATIONAL MOTOR MUSEUM

Three TR-X prototypes were built, of which two are believed to survive. KHP 712 is shown here at a Club event held at Bletchley Park, England, in 2000.
RON CROMAR, TRIUMPH ROADSTER CLUB

of TR until the arrival of the TR5 much later in the story. With the engine change, as well as the model designation being modified to 20TR from the original 18TR, a new three-speed gearbox was fitted. The Renown went through similar changes, as well as subtle modifications to the bodywork that added length. The next saloon model was to be the Standard Vanguard. Its major contribution to the TR story was its engine, which had first been used in the earlier Triumphs.

Only 4,501 examples of the Triumph Roadster were produced up to the end of production in September 1949. Its replacement, styled by Walter Belgrove, was code-named 'TR-X'. Three prototypes were completed before the car was shown at the Paris and London Motor Shows of 1950. Despite numerous unique features and a very high specification, it had a mixed reception. Perhaps this was for the best, as its styling shared similar overall concepts with its contemporary, the Austin Atlantic, which had not had the success that had been originally hoped. Jaguar had launched the striking XK120 and, with that, a new design motif for the 1950s was becoming established. The rethink that followed TR-X led rapidly to 20TS and, from that, to TR2.

THE FIRST TR

Sir John Black had an ambition to build and sell a sports car. His approach to Jaguar for a joint project had been thwarted and attempts to absorb the Morgan Company, to whom Standard continued to supply engines, had been rebuffed. Meanwhile, MG were selling every vehicle they could build, low-volume production companies such as Jowett and Allard were enjoying success in a market space that was seen as being the natural home for Triumph, and even Austin was having some success with their A40 Sports.

An edict was issued that a 2-litre Triumph sports car with a top speed of around 90mph (140km/h) and a target price of £500 plus purchase tax would be on display at the 1952 Motor Show to be held in October at Earls Court in London. Walter Belgrove was to be responsible for the styling while Harry Webster was to look after the mechanical aspects. The front suspension and steering were taken from the Triumph Mayflower, a small two-door monocoque saloon car with styling similar to the Renown, and the rear axle was again similar to that of the Mayflower, but reduced in width to suit the new design. The chassis was based on a pre-war Standard Flying Nine, a stock of which had been found in store. The axle was mounted above the chassis side rails, a decision that was to have serious consequences before long. The engine was the wet-liner type common across the company's product range, but fitted with liners to bring the capacity to 1991cc, ensuring that the car could compete in the under 2-litre class in motorsport. The gearbox came from the Vanguard, but with the addition of an extra speed and a remote linkage to give a gear change totally in keeping with a modern sports car.

THE TRACTOR CONNECTION

One of the most numerous implementations of the Standard wet-liner engine was as the power plant for the fabled 'little grey Fergie' tractor. It was a vehicle that made a significant contribution to agricultural industrialization in the 1950s and is now preserved as a favourite power source for ploughing competitions.

Its war-time efforts in building equipment and munitions had left Standard with a liability in the form of the Banner Lane plant, which no longer fitted in with the company's plans, as long as the two plants at Canley and Fletchampstead were more than adequate to cope with the activities planned for the foreseeable future. The issue with Banner Lane was that the lease was such that Black was unwilling to surrender it. The question therefore was what should be done with it. The answer came in the form of Harry Ferguson, who had designed and was promoting a lightweight agricultural tractor, along with a revolutionary linkage system bearing his name that provided for the easy interchange of equipment.

In 1945, seeing the huge expansion in mechanized farming, Ferguson was holding discussions with third parties who might be in a position to manufacture the tractor, provided that Ferguson retained the sales rights. Talks with Lord Nuffield and Sir Leonard Lord had been inconclusive, but once Sir John Black was made aware through various contacts of Ferguson's need, a deal was struck. Standard-Triumph would build the tractors at Banner Lane – the overall group manufacturing overheads could be amortized over a larger production volume and the tractors would be fitted with a version of Standard's new wet-liner 4-cylinder engine. It was an arrangement that would lead many years later to much banter between TR drivers and enthusiasts of other marques, with TRs sometimes accused of being fitted with 'tractor engines'.

Ferguson and Black were both single-minded businessmen, quite convinced of the value of their own judgement. As a result, their relationship was defined by differences of opinion and arguments, as Colin Fraser affirmed in his biography of Ferguson (*Harry Ferguson: Inventor and Pioneer*): 'Both men were inflexible and aggressively certain that their opinions were infallibly right'. Nevertheless, even though the whole relationship was founded on nothing more than a gentleman's handshake, the business proved valuable to both parties even after Ferguson merged with the Canadian company Massey-Harris at the end of 1953.

Meanwhile, work continued on the styling. From the rear wheels forward, the style is immediately familiar and unmistakably a TR, while the rear of the car had a distinctive style reminiscent of the contemporary Morgan Plus 4. This brought several disadvantages: the fuel tank was positioned behind the rear axle, the spare wheel was mounted externally with the filler spout for the fuel tank protruding through its centre, and there was no luggage space. The target cost for design was not met, being slightly more than 10 per cent higher, at £555. Purchase tax took the total price to £865.

The little car was formally designated '20TS', but over time it has become known as the TR1, although this was never an official title.

On the very same day of the announcement of the Triumph sports car to the public, news of the car that was to be manufactured as the Austin-Healey 100 also came through.

THE BIRTH OF THE TR ■

THE WET-LINER ENGINE

The Standard wet-liner engine found numerous applications in many capacities and states of tune, from the Ferguson 'Little Grey Fergie' tractor to rally-winning TR4s. First used in 2088cc format in the later Triumph Roadster models and throughout the Vanguard series, perhaps the most successful application was in the TR. The advantage of wet liners, in addition to the increased cooling area and ease of future maintenance, was the simplicity of changing the bore and thus the engine capacity. With a stroke of 92mm, the Vanguard bore of 85mm gave a capacity of 2088cc, but in the case of the TR installation, modifying the liners to give an 83mm bore reduced the capacity to 1991cc, conveniently fitting the car into the 2-litre capacity class for competition. For its time, the stroke was short; one result of the RAC HP rating for taxation purposes was a tendency among designers to produce long-stroke engines, which, while able to develop large amounts of torque, were slow to 'rev' and not suitable for a sports car. The short stroke made engine speeds of 5,000rpm possible. Similarly, a compression ratio of 8.5:1 was prescribed, along with a cross-drilled, three-bearing crank. The earliest engines built went without the cross-drilling to the crank. Bearings were of the modern shell type. Both inlet and exhaust manifolds were fitted to the left side of the engine (when viewed from the front), although photographs of the Vanguard engine fitted in the prototype TR-X show the inlet manifold on the right side, giving a crossflow configuration, a set-up that was not used on other implementations. The exhaust was subject to detail modifications of length and silencer configuration before the definitive system was obtained, along with its very distinctive exhaust note.

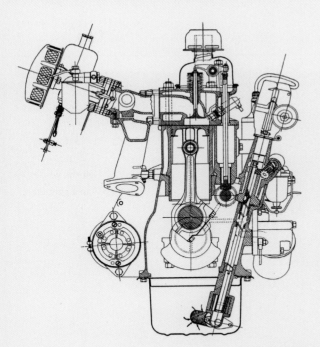
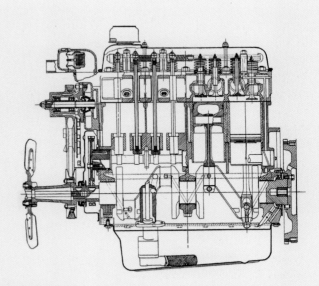

Engineering general assembly diagrams of the 4-cylinder wet-liner engine used with great success by Standard-Triumph across the product range but particularly in TRs. An original of this image adorns the board room of the TR Register.
TR REGISTER ARCHIVE COLLECTION/ © BMIHT

continued overleaf

Illustration of the TR engine used in the sales brochures for TRs during the 1950s.
© BMIHT

The 20TS was shown to the public for the first time at the London Motor Show in 1952.
© BMIHT

INITIAL REACTIONS

The first reactions to the appearance of the 20TS centred on the rear of the car. There was no luggage space and the design was unappealing. After the Earls Court Show, a small, select group of motoring journalists were permitted a test drive, but reviews were not good. There were concerns about the road-holding, the ride, which was firm even for a sports car, and flexing of the chassis.

Seeking an outside opinion, the company invited the well-known racing car designer and tester Ken Richardson to drive the 20TS and report his findings. Richardson at the time was working on the V-16 engined Formula One car for BRM. Unfortunately, he agreed with the motoring journalists, describing the 20TS variously as 'the most awful car I have

ever driven' and 'a death trap'. The direction that history takes often depends on a single decision. In this case, Sir John Black could have persevered with the original design, citing cost issues as a reason not to make any significant changes; in all likelihood, the car would have been a commercial disaster, and might even have marked the end of the line for the Triumph name. His other option was to hear and respond to the feedback proffered and use it to improve the car. Triumph enthusiasts will be thankful that he chose to take the second route.

Ken Richardson was invited to join the development team, in conjunction with Harry Webster as chief chassis engineer and Walter Belgrove in charge of the bodywork. Richardson's expertise in testing and development was brought to the fore with this project.

'The most awful car I have ever driven,' according to Ken Richardson, 20TS sits on trade plates while undergoing testing as part of the redesign that would lead to the TR2.

© BMIHT

HARRY WEBSTER CBE

© BMIHT

Henry George Webster, always known as Harry, was born in Coventry in 1917 and studied at the local technical college before joining 'The Standard' as an engineering apprentice at the age of fifteen. The war years saw him working in inspection on aircraft engines in one of the shadow factories operated by Standard, prior to returning to chassis design in 1945. Rising rapidly through the ranks, by 1948 Webster was chief chassis engineer and a core member of the team that developed the TR2. Appointed Director of Engineering in 1957, Webster was key to the product success of Triumph, producing all the successful models that were to carry the Triumph name, working in an environment where cash was tightly limited.

Perhaps his most significant achievement at that time was recognizing the talent of Giovanni Michelotti, whose styling designs set Triumph apart from its competitors. It was under the leadership of Webster, an enthusiast for motorsport, that Triumph was to achieve success at Le Mans with the TRS.

Following the merger between Leyland and British Motor Holdings in 1968, to form British Leyland, Webster was moved to the volume car division based at the former Austin plant at Longbridge. There he faced two immediate difficulties. First, there was a need to replace the legendary Alec Issigonis, who had been moved to head research projects; the second was to untangle the muddle of the product range, where it was hoped that the sparkle of the Triumph name might spread to the volume market. The structure, the political environment and not least the poor industrial relations meant that, even with the colossal abilities of Webster, the plan to emulate the product-led strategies of Ford came to nothing. Webster left British Leyland in 1974, the year he was appointed CBE, for a position as Group Technical Director with component supplier Automotive Products, before retiring in 1982.

He recalled his experiences with British Leyland, saying, 'If you're in business, whether you're making furniture or selling fish and chips, you're doing it to make money, to make a profit. If you don't, you go to the wall. I'm not sentimental about cars.'

Harry Webster died in February 2007. Always a well-respected engineer and manager, he was to become an important personality for enthusiasts when the cars for which he was responsible achieved cherished classic status. He is honoured today by a grouping of Standard-Triumph car clubs that have named an annual award in his memory.

20TS EVOLVES INTO TR2

The new design provided a more rigid chassis, with enhanced stiffening in the central cruciform, and larger brakes. A change in the valve arrangements and an increase in the compression ratio increased the engine output from 75bhp to 90bhp, which was quite respectable for the time. The new engine output figure was significant as it matched

The rolling chassis of the new revised TR2, as illustrated in the sales brochure.
© BMIHT

that of the Austin-Healey 100 that had been announced at the same time as the 20TS at the London Motor Show. There was one major difference, though: the Healey's Austin engine required 2660cc capacity to equal the power developed by the Triumph's 1991cc.

The most obvious changes were to the bodywork. The flat windscreen was given a gentle curve, the sidelights were moved from the wing tops to the front of the car and, significantly, the rear quarter was redesigned. Where the original design gave no luggage space and an externally mounted spare wheel, Belgrove's revision provided for a sweeping tail, with the fuel tank now positioned above the rear axle, a proper luggage boot and housing for a spare wheel in its own compartment, accessed by a removable cover located below the boot opening. In this general form, the car would become familiar – with detail changes – for the next ten years. The new car was first seen in public at the Geneva Motor Show in March 1953.

LEFT: **OHP 242** was a very early-build TR2 used for promotional purposes. Seen here in a traditional English country setting with Ken Richardson at the wheel.
© BMIHT VIA NATIONAL MOTOR MUSEUM

BELOW: **OHP 242** survives to this day and is seen here in company with 773 EWO, better known by its commission number of TS2, the first production right-hand-drive TR2.

Triumph TR2: Original Specification

Layout and Chassis
Two-seat sports car with separate chassis

Engine

Type	Standard-Triumph 'wet-liner'
Block material	Cast iron
Head material	Cast iron
Cylinders	4 in-line
Cooling	Water
Bore and stroke	83mm bore, 92mm stroke
Capacity	1991cc
Valves	2 valves per cylinder ohv
Compression ratio	8.5:1
Carburettor	2 SU H4
Max. power	90bhp @ 4,800rpm
Max. torque	117lb ft @ 3,000rpm
Fuel capacity	12.5 gallons (56.8 litres)

Transmission

Clutch	Single dry plate, hydraulic actuation
Gearbox	S-T 4-speed with synchromesh on top 3 speeds
Ratios	
1st	4.28:1
2nd	2.00:1
3rd	1.325:1
4th	1.00:1
Overdrive (optional, top gear only on early cars; 2nd, 3rd and top otherwise)	0.82:1
Reverse	4.28:1
Final drive	3.7:1

Suspension and Steering

Front	Independent using unequal-length wishbones, coil springs and telescopic dampers
Rear	Live axle, half-elliptical leaf springs, lever-arm dampers
Steering	Cam and lever steering box
Tyres	5.50 – 15 inch crossply
Wheels	Pressed-steel disc wheels with 4-stud fixing. Optional centre-lock wire wheels
Rim width	4 inches

Brakes

Type	Drums, front and rear
Size	
Front:	10 × 2.25 inches
Rear:	9.0 × 1.75 inches

Dimensions

Track	
Front	45 inches (1,145mm)
Rear	45.5 inches (1,160mm)
Wheelbase	88 inches (2,235mm)
Overall length	151 inches (3,840mm)
Overall width	55.5 inches (1,410mm)
Overall height	50.5 inches (1,280mm)
Unladen weight	1,981lb (902kg)

Performance

Top speed	107.3mph (173km/h) (*Motor*, 1954)
0–60mph	11.9 sec (*Motor*, 1954)

EARLY MARKET COMPETITORS

Donald Healey showed his Healey 100 sports car at Earls Court in 1952 alongside the 20TS. During the course of the show, the legendary agreement was made between Healey and Leonard Lord of Austin for the car to be manufactured by that company, giving rise to the sales launch of the car as the 'Austin-Healey 100'. Lord's intervention allowed the target launch price to be reduced by a full £100. The Rootes Group had introduced the Sunbeam Alpine in 1953 and the buyer in search of a traditional British sports car might also consider the MG range. In 1953, the long-standing model TD was about to be supplanted by the new TF, but not until the end of the year. How did the Triumph compare with its contemporaries?

In terms of performance achieved for money spent, Standard-Triumph appeared to have a winner on their hands. They had a design that was attractive and a performance that was the equal of cars costing half as much again – a fundamental feature that was to stay with the TR range until the demise of the marque, an event that was still a long way in the future. Production deliveries were scheduled for July 1953, with the first two pre-production cars, TS1, a left-hand-drive model, and TS2, in right-hand-drive form, being completed on 22 July. Both cars featured a number of detail

TRIUMPH TR2 – THE COMPETITORS

	Triumph TR2	Austin-Healey 100	Sunbeam Alpine	MG TD
Engine capacity	1991cc	2660cc	2267cc	1250cc
Max. power	90bhp @ 4,800rpm	90bhp @ 4,000rpm	80bhp @ 4,200rpm	54bhp @ 5,200rpm
Max. torque	117lb ft @ 3,000rpm	144lb ft @ 2,500rpm	124lb ft @ 1,800rpm	64lb ft @ 2,600rpm
Top speed	107mph	115mph	95mph	80mph
0–60mph	11.9 sec	10.3 sec	18.9 sec	23.5 sec
Price in 1953	£555	£750	£895	£585

Although the Sunbeam Alpine hardly has the appearance of a sports car, it did have a successful rallying career and was something that the prospective purchaser of a TR might consider in 1953.

The MG Midget T series of cars changed little. Although this particular model is a TC and dates from 1949, very little changed in the general design of the cars and it would have been an interesting proposition to consider second-hand if the budget did not stretch to a new TR2.

differences from the volume production cars that were to follow.

The launch of the car had been quite spectacular. Neighbouring Coventry manufacturer Rootes had sent their new Sunbeam Alpine to the Jabekke highway in Belgium for a demonstration speed run. Not being one to miss an opportunity, Sir John Black arranged for Ken Richardson to take the third prototype TR2, commission number X519, to Belgium to match and preferably beat the speed set by the Sunbeam. The car was registered as MVC 575 and subtly modified by the addition of rear-wheel spats and a full-length under shield. A metal tonneau cover was fitted, the wind-

screen was replaced with a small aero screen and bumpers were removed before the car was taken to Belgium for the speed attempt. On 20 May 1953 a speed of 104.86mph (168.7km/h) was achieved, but it was quickly discovered that this had been with the engine running on just three cylinders. A subsequent attempt with the engine running on all four cylinders gave a top speed of 124.889mph (200.945km/h). The TR2 had achieved, as Raymond Baxter commentated in a contemporary Standard-Triumph film unit production, not only 'what had been planned – the fastest under 2-litre sports car of its price', but also the setting of a world record for a 2-litre sports car.

ABOVE: **TS2 is now held in trust by the TR Register and sees regular use to promote the TR marque. The car was originally shipped to Ireland.**

LEFT: **From time to time, TS2 ventures back to Ireland, where it is reunited with its original registration. The original weather equipment as fitted here lacked rear quarter 'windows', seriously limiting visibility and making driving in modern traffic conditions difficult.**

With the car in 'speed trim', Ken Richardson prepares to tackle the Jabekke Straight, setting the world speed record for a sub-2-litre car.
© BMIHT

Steve Harridge has owned this early long-door TR2 for over forty years. It is shown in the New Forest just after returning from a trip to Tuscany – quite an achievement for a sixty-two-year-old car.

CHAPTER THREE

THE SIDE SCREEN ERA

The Triumph TR 'side screen' cars become a worldwide success. The model evolves, with almost continual product enhancement, from its introduction in 1953 to the end of the manufacturing of side-screen cars in 1962, when the TR3B finally ceases production.

Despite the TR2 setting records for its class at Jabekke, production began at a crawl. In the 1950s, Standard-Triumph were purchasing parts and sub-assemblies from various suppliers, all brought together as a car at the Canley Works. The chassis was constructed in Wellington, Shropshire by Sankey. Initially, raw pressings were supplied to Canley where assembly was completed, but, after about 1,400 cars had been built, Sankey installed their own assembly jigs and completed chassis were supplied. Body shells were built by Mulliners of Birmingham, later acquired by Standard-Triumph; electrical systems (of course) were provided by Lucas; front suspension and steering came from Alford & Adler, another business that was eventually brought in-house; and scores of suppliers provided other individual components. To complicate matters further, 1953 saw a significant product range revision with the introduction of the new Standard 8 replacing the Triumph Mayflower. Slightly fewer than 250 cars were shipped during 1953.

TR FINDS ITS MARKET

Autocar published a flattering road-test report on the new car in January 1954. If the motoring press could be convinced that Standard-Triumph had produced a winner, the public might agree and the car would be a success in its market. With expectations somewhat low, based on reactions to the Triumph Roadster of the late 1940s, a geranium-coloured car fitted with overdrive – the sixth

to be produced and registered as OHP 771 – was made available for testing in late 1953. In March 1954, the same car was loaned to journalists at *Autocar*'s rival title *Motor*, whose report was equally positive, although perhaps a little less effusive. In the specialist media, *Autosport* were equally positive, going so far as to say, 'if you see that low, blunt nose in your mirror, pull over and let him go, unless you have something very hot!' Bill Boddy, writing in *Motor Sport* a year later, was of the opinion that 'this already firmly established sports model clearly has a rosy future ahead of it'. In the United States, a reporter writing in *Road & Track* in April 1954 was convinced that 'the TR2 [would] out-drag any stock American car from a standstill'. Praise indeed.

Sporting success came early: in the 1954 RAC Rally, John Wallwork finished as outright winner, with Peter Cooper second and Mary Walker winning the Coupe des Dames. Fourteen TR2s had started and only one car failed to finish. For a car that had been on sale for only a matter of months, the results were nothing short of spectacular and did not go unnoticed by motorsport enthusiasts. Production was soon increased to 100 cars per week.

The early cars were subjected to a number of detail design changes during the early production phases. To the outsider, the most obvious would have been a reduction of the distinctive exhaust rasp, as a result of the fitting of a longer silencer. Another distinctive change was the substitution of the original aluminium bonnet with one pressed in steel.

Standard-Triumph cars are identified by what is known as a 'commission number', which in modern terms would be called the VIN number. Commission numbers comprise a two- or three-letter prefix designating the model type, a numeric sequence and a suffix identifying factory-fitted options, such as overdrive. The prefix letters used for the side screen cars are 'TS', often thought to stand for 'TRIUMPH SPORTS'.

Certain cars are best known by their commission numbers, particularly the earliest cars, TS1 and TS2.

The 'TS' indicative prefix was unique to side screen cars, with other combinations of letters being allocated to later models until the universal application of the new scheme was introduced towards the end of TR7 production.

LONG DOORS VERSUS SHORT DOORS

The original design featured doors that extended below the sills. This had the distinct disadvantage that, when the car was parked, the door adjacent to a kerb could not be opened without risk of damage against the kerb – sometimes it could not be opened at all. TR enthusiasts refer to these early cars as 'long-door cars'. A redesign at the end of 1953 led to the doors being shortened and external sills fitted from October 1954 – the delay resulting from the time necessary to produce new press tools and assembly jigs. The first of the revised cars bore the commission number TS4002. Naturally enough, these later cars are referred to as 'short-door cars'.

More detail changes followed. In 1955, the rear brakes were revised, increasing the drum size to 10 inches (250mm), and the overdrive was revised to function on all but bottom gear, thus giving, at least in theory, seven forward ratios. The overdrive switch became a toggle switch

The long door covered the car's sill, but was susceptible to damage against kerbs.

A rapid redesign led to the short door that was fitted to later cars to overcome the problem.

instead of the original pull switch; it was still mounted on the dashboard, but now easily operated with a flick of the hand. An electrical interlocking arrangement prevented overdrive being engaged in first or reverse gear. Externally, a new design of soft top was provided, with rear quarter windows, dramatically improving visibility. A factory hard top was also made available. At about the same time, the original bonnet-release mechanism was replaced with a set of budget locks operated using the same tee key required to open the boot.

ABOVE LEFT: **TR2s were fitted with a comprehensive set of instruments in a layout that hardly changed from the first TR2 to the last TR6.**

ABOVE RIGHT: **Seating was well up to the standards of the mid-1950s, although three-point seat belts were something for the future. The transmission tunnel was kept clear of obstructions, with the gear level positioned well forward under the dashboard and the handbrake located in the driver's footwell.**

ABOVE LEFT: **Rear lighting was, quite typically for the early 1950s, very simple. A central stop light also served to illuminate the number plate, and there were combined tail lamps and turn signals. The spare wheel was stored in the compartment behind the number plate.**

ABOVE RIGHT: **Wet-weather gear consisted of side screens and a cover erected over a simple frame.**

ABOVE: **Prepared to face the weather with side screens fitted and roof in place. TR2s are not entirely watertight and water seems to find its way in under and around the windscreen. The zips in the side screens provide access to the cords inside used to open the doors. Security locks to the doors would not be fitted until much later.**

LEFT: **The front edge of the rear wing was identified as being susceptible to damage. A factory-fitted polished cover plate minimized the risk of stone chips.**

THE TR2: CURRENT OWNERS' PERSPECTIVES

Michael Eatough's 'little car'.

Michael Eatough owns a 1955-built TR2, restored and maintained in near-original condition, among an eclectic collection of classic cars that includes several Porsches, an Austin A35 van and a Mercedes 'fin-tail' endurance rally car. Although it is a 60-year-old car, Michael's TR2 is regularly used, including a tour of Greece within the past ten years, involving daily journeys of around 350 miles in Mediterranean summer temperatures. The 'little car', as Michael often refers to it, is not perfect but is maintained to keep it in the same condition as a typical car of its era and is extensively used in the drier months as an everyday car for local use. All the mechanicals are original, with drum brakes and steering box, but it is quite capable of making progress alongside modern traffic both in the town and on the open road.

The car was acquired almost by accident. Michael says that he attended an auction with a friend who was interested in bidding on a Morgan, similar to one that Michael already owned. The Morgan was not purchased, but towards the end of the day's sale the TR2 appeared in the ring. It was being bid up in small increments by a couple of potential buyers who were seemingly not that enthusiastic about actually purchasing.

Almost at the final fall of the hammer, Michael entered his bid and won. He sold the Morgan soon after. 'The problem with the Morgan', he says, 'was that it was really a modern car with none of the comforts or benefits and while it looked like a classic car, it wasn't and so was not eligible for any classic car events.'

Michael had not inspected the car prior to the auction, so he contacted the seller, an established classic car dealer in Kent, to find out a little about it and the reasons for selling. There was nothing to worry about – the car was in good overall condition, there were no hidden secrets, and it had only been entered in the auction to move it on and generate some cash flow for the seller. Along with the car came a factory hard top and almost the complete service history.

Does the car have any drawbacks? The side screens have never fitted properly and rain does get in around them and below the windscreen. The boot is rather small so, when touring, the choice has to be whether to take luggage or the side screens. Luggage usually wins. The hard top is exceptionally heavy, so it is stored safely and not used. And the optional factory-fitted heater is a little feeble and struggles to demist the screen.

continued overleaf

THE TR2: CURRENT OWNERS' PERSPECTIVES *continued*

Steve Harridge owns an earlier 'long-door' TR2 that has been subject over the past sixty years to numerous minor enhancements to improve its comfort in modern driving. Steve has owned the car from the early 1970s and has used it as his daily driver until quite recently, showing that older cars can be reliable in daily use. In the summer of 2015, the car was transport for Steve and his wife Sue for a holiday to Tuscany, dealing with the altitude of Alpine passes, busy *autostrade* and high summer temperatures without any problems.

'George', Steve Harridge's early long-door TR2. When in daily use, a large toy dragon was regularly carried as a passenger, hence the name.

In the first two years of production, to the end of 1954, over 5,000 TRs were sold with over 70 per cent of production being exported, predominantly to the United States. Purchasers could specify numerous options for their car, with centre-lock painted wire wheels being a common feature. The rear wheel arch spats, as featured on the Jabekke speed trial car, were another option, but they were rarely fitted and not possible at all with wire wheels because the centre spinners would foul on the covers. Later, in 1955, the TR2 underwent a further series of improvements and was renamed TR3.

The TR2 sales brochure: very much a product of its time.
© BMIHT

INTRODUCING TR3

With the introduction of the TR3, there was a change to the front-end visual styling of Standard-Triumph cars, which had been established with the introduction of the Vanguard immediately after the end of the Second World War. In place of the 'open-mouth' appearance, a new grille was fitted at the front of the opening, creating a distinctive up-to-date appearance, and providing a very simple method

of differentiating between a TR2 and a TR3. At least, it would have been had it not been for the habit of owners to modify their cars in period to give the appearance of the latest model. Cosmetically, the painted hinges fitted to the TR2 were now chromed and the bead seal along the wings changed from body colour to stainless steel. One new accessory for the TR3 was an occasional rear seat, really only suitable for a small person, in those far-off days when it was considered quite normal to carry children

Detail changes can be seen on this perfect example of an early TR3 – new grille cover, stainless-steel beading, chromed hinges and sliding windows in the side screens.

unrestrained in the rear of cars. This required a modification to the front seats to allow the backs to fold for access into the rear compartment. A more useful change was the addition of sliding sections to the weather-screen sides, providing some ventilation.

Power output was increased to 95bhp by specifying 1¾ inch SU carburettors and a new design of cylinder head based on experience gained in competition. Almost immediately, further changes to the engine were implemented. Following Triumph's success in the 1955 twenty-four-hour event at Le Mans, the production cars received a modified version of the cylinder head used in the race cars. This was rapidly followed by a new casting for the cylinder head, producing what became known as the 'high port' head and increasing the performance of the engine to a true 100bhp.

Nominally designed as an 'occasional' seat for children, the rear seat could be used by adults only for very short journeys. The black webbing straps are from the roof frame structure, not seat belts.

Sliding perspex windows are now fitted into the side screens, providing for better ventilation and easier access to open the door.

The simple but efficient dashboard was not changed from the TR2. The 'fly-off' handbrake was positioned close to the driver's left leg, while the overdrive switch was located at the extreme right edge of the dashboard.

A very tidy engine bay, complete with 1955-style battery. Production cars would not normally be fitted with a chromed rocker cover, but, as this car was prepared for the 1955 Motor Show, it is likely to have been subject to extra care and attention.

WKK 567 – A 1955 MOTOR SHOW SURVIVOR

Ben Wood's exceptionally well restored and preserved former London Motor Show TR3.

Standard Register

Extract from the production records of The Standard Motor Company Limited.

Commission No:	TS 8703'O'
Type:	TR3
Building Date:	Thursday, 22nd September 1955. 7.30–9.30am
Body Shell No:	841257
Tyre Size:	550
Body Colour:	Pearl White
Trim Colour & Type:	Blue Leather
Hood/Side Curtains Colour:	Fawn/–
Delivery Destination:	Earls Court Motor Show No21
Other Specifications and Equipment:	R M H h 'O' ORS
Special Notes:	Manifold and Carburettor to be changed

for codes see reverse

The build record suggests that the car was actually built as a TR2 with the engine modified to TR3 specification prior to shipment to Earls Court.

Built on Thursday 22 September 1955 and delivered directly to Stand 21 at Earls Court, TS8703 was one of two new TR3 cars displayed by Mulliners at the 1955 London Motor Show as a convertible. (The other was shown with a fitted hard top.) Now owned by Ben Wood, the car has been restored to a very high condition of originality retaining the as-built Pearl White coachwork, blue leather interior and fawn hood and side screens.

The car's build record shows the interesting instruction 'Manifold and carburettor [sic] to be changed', suggesting that the car was originally constructed as a late model TR2 and converted to a TR3 prior to shipment. Although it was not a standard fitting on production cars, WKK also sports a chromed rocker cover. It is reasonable to assume that this would have been fitted to show off the car at Earls Court.

After being found in a shed in the Midlands, the car was comprehensively restored and re-registered in 2009 and acquired by Ben Wood in 2013, his first classic car following on from a passion for classic British motorcycles – Triumphs, naturally. There are a small number of deviations from the original specification: a high-torque starter motor is fitted and the rear axle is the later TR3A style, although Ben is intending to replace this with the genuine TR2/TR3 item when one can be located. Maintenance is sympathetic with the age and history of the car. When shown in 1955, the car was fitted with steel wheels; today these are interchanged with a painted spoked set.

The original tool kit remains with Ben Wood's car.

A BREAKTHROUGH IN BRAKING

Triumph's reputation for innovation and bringing race-circuit technology to the sort of car that the typical customer could purchase was firmly established from October 1956, when disc brakes became a standard fitting on the TR3. Previous cars had used a Lockheed braking set-up, an arrangement that was quite typical of its time. Increasing speeds and traffic densities created a mar-

From the TR3 brochure. Throughout the 1950s, Triumph's marketing department commissioned high-quality sketches and paintings to illustrate its publicity material.

© BMIHT

ket opportunity for more effective braking, copying the benefits that had been seen on the motorsport circuits. Disc-brake technology had been implemented for bespoke circuit cars, but Triumph's fit to the 1955 Le Mans cars was a first use of disc brakes on production sports cars. For the 1957 model year, the TR3 was delivered fitted with disc brakes and a revised rear axle derived from that being fitted to the Standard Vanguard III saloon car. Triumph's lead in this area was maintained for around two years until the rival MGA and Austin-Healey were given front disc brakes, but it was the little Triumph that had again set new standards.

AN EARLY TR3?

Although originally purchased to use as a competition car, David Erskine's TR3 provides sterling service as wedding transport.

David Erskine owns an early TR3, built on 23 November 1955 and first registered in January 1956. He acquired the car in 1972 with the intention of owning it for sprint racing. It quickly became apparent that the car was not original; the factory-fitted engine had been replaced with that from a Standard Vanguard. In the early 1970s older TRs were seen as ideal cars for club motorsport and there was little concern about authenticity. Every year the car has been modified to improve on the previous year, until, as David says, 'the performance of the car began to exceed my own…'.

Even on close inspection, the car appears to be an authentic early TR3, but under closer examination the modifications come to light: TR4 engine, TR6 gearbox, TR3A rear axle and rack and pinion steering and TR6 disc brakes. The original rear turn indicators and central brake lights have been modified in the interest of road safety. Quickly removable orange turn signals have been fitted on top of the rear over-riders, replacing the original red indicators within the tail marker lights. These now operate as combined tail and brake lights while the original central brake light still operates in keeping with the central light now fitted to modern vehicles. Race-car seats and a Mota-Lita steering wheel, plus a rollover bar give away the car's sporting history and performance.

continued overleaf

AN EARLY TR3? *continued*

When driving in Europe, following motorists expect turn signals to be amber, not red, as originally fitted by Triumph. David Erskine has fitted an easily removable modification to his TR3, using fittings from a Honda motorcycle, and rewired the red lamps so that all three red lamps will illuminate when the brake pedal is pressed.

LEFT: **Later production models of TR3s had a revision made to the rear lights to incorporate separate flashing orange turn signals.**

Triumph TR3 – Revised Specification

As TR2 except as noted below:

Engine
Carburettor   2 SU H6
Max. power   95bhp @ 4,800rpm
                100bhp @ 5,000rpm with high-port head
Max. torque   117lb ft @ 3,000rpm

Brakes
Type   Drums, front and rear

From commission No. TS13046: disc, front; drums, rear
Size
     Drum-braked cars – as TR2
     Disc-braked cars: 11 inch diameter discs at front, 10 x 2.25
                 inch at rear

Performance
Top speed   105.3mph (169.5km/h) (*Motor*, 1956 – tested
                with hard top fitted)
0–60mph   10.8 sec (*Motor*, 1956)

A TR FOR THE CHILDREN

Sports cars have always been attractive to children and TRs are no exception. When asked what he might like for his fifth birthday present in 1960, David Hunt's son asked for a pedal car, one like a friend's father's car, perhaps? His friend's father's car happened to be a new TR3A. From that suggestion emerged a one-third near-scale replica TR3A pedal car that was to become the foundation of a new business, which was to go on to produce over 100 examples.

In an article first published in the TR Register magazine *TR Action* (April 2013), David Hunt recalls how, having built the first prototype and deciding to enter into limited production of about five 'cars' in total, to offset the expenses incurred, he thought it might be prudent to seek the approval of Standard-Triumph to avoid any TR design copyright issues. He produced several photographs of the model and sent these to Canley.

Within a very short space of time, no more than a week, a telephone conversation ensued between David and the PR & Marketing Department of Standard-Triumph. In contrast to the awkward 'cease and desist' notice that might have been

expected, the project was met with great enthusiasm and a meeting was hastily arranged for the model to be examined. As a result of the meeting, David was asked whether he could 'make a bigger one, say half-size, that two children could pedal'. And would he be able to handle the production of 100 such models? Funding was established via David's employer at the time, a new company set up, premises found and production advice sought and obtained, with expertise brought in from the aerospace industry.

Production ran at four cars per week and these were delivered to Canley on, naturally, a half-scale car transporter. Standard-Triumph produced an official sales brochure in their house style for distribution by dealers. Some of the cars have survived and one is displayed at the British Motor Industry Heritage Trust's Museum at Gaydon in Warwickshire. It was restored by David himself after his son, for whom the original model was created, found it in the garden of a property he visited while searching for a full-scale TR3 to purchase. The find was made some twenty-five years after the model had first been created.

TRs have an appeal for all ages.
DAVID HUNT

continued overleaf

A TR FOR THE CHILDREN *continued*

As production of the pedal cars expanded, the obvious method to transport the finished product was a scale car transporter, seen here towed by a TR3A.
DAVID HUNT

Side-screen cars were fitted as standard with these disc wheels and chromed hub caps featuring the Triumph globe badge. As a concours entrant, this owner has ensured that the car has been parked with the badge the correct way up.

THE TR3 GAINS A 'GRINNING GRILLE'

January 1958 saw the public launch of a further revised TR3 that became immediately known as the TR3A, although the designation was not used officially until much later. The new car could be easily identified from its predecessors by the new wide front grille. Less obvious was the addition of locking door handles and a key-operated boot lid, although carriage locks still secured the spare-wheel cover and bonnet, so a budget key was still an essential item to be carried in the car. A further subtle change to the frontal aspect of the car resulted in the headlights becoming slightly recessed into the apron of the car and the manufacturer's name being added beneath the Standard-Triumph badge.

Although production of the new car had commenced in the third quarter of the previous year, the public launch was held back to allow substantial stocks to be delivered

RIGHT: **The frontal view of the TR3A is easily identifiable, with its wide 'grinning grille' and the addition of the Triumph name to the front apron.**

BELOW LEFT: **A detailed examination of the headlight pods fitted to a TR2 or TR3 shows that they protrude forward of the front apron line ...**

BELOW RIGHT: **... whereas, for the TR3A, the modified shape of the car's new front to incorporate the full-width grille dictated that the headlights would be recessed very slightly into the apron.**

ABOVE: **A lockable boot lid was also fitted to the TR3A, but the spare-wheel cover still required a tee key to operate its budget locks.**

LEFT: **TR3A finally gets external door handles and a key-operated lock. It looks slightly unusual, but the rear-facing fitting is correct.**

An obvious showroom competitor to the TR3A, the MGA. This example dates from towards the end of the production run of just over 100,000 cars of which only 5,800 were sold into the home market.

to dealers, particularly in the United States, where sales of TRs were booming. The TR had always been a success in export markets and from 1956 until the end of production, export sales contributed significantly to the balance of payments. In 1958, for example, of almost 16,000 cars delivered, just 500 or so were for the home market. To misquote British Prime Minister Harold MacMillan, it was a period when the motor industry, and Triumph especially, had 'never had it so good'.

The TR3A at the time was competing in the showrooms with the evolving 'Big' Healey and with the MGA. By 1956, the Healey had been fitted with a 6-cylinder BMC C-series engine, initially of 2.6 litres capacity and increasing to 2.9 litres in 1958, thus putting the car into a different class. The MGA was priced competitively against the Triumph, but did not achieve the same success in motorsport and perhaps appealed to a different sector of the market. A high-perfor-

mance MGA was introduced with a twin-cam engine, which was to give rise to a set of reliability issues that Triumph itself was to experience some eight years later following the introduction of petrol injection. Curiously, the issues in both cases that so badly damaged the reputation of both manufacturers have now been almost entirely overcome as the cars have evolved into cherished classics.

A final set of detail modifications followed during 1959. After some 41,000 TR2 and TR3 bodies had been produced, a new set of press tools was completed, to replace the original set that had been in use since 1953. Commission number TS60001 was the first car to be built using the new tools and they were to continue in use, producing a further 38,000 bodies. Various production improvements were implemented, but the only obvious change was to the areas around the hinges to the boot, where a raised 'land' was incorporated for the hinge baseplate.

BIGGER ENGINES

With the 1991cc engine fitted to the TR, the car fitted neatly into the 2-litre class for motorsport. The obvious advantage of using wet liners meant that increasing the engine bore was a relatively simple matter and similar engines of 2088cc capacity were in common use as the motor for the current Standard Vanguard from 1947 through to 1961. The Ferguson tractor, using fundamentally the same engine, was provided with a capacity of 2188cc.

In 1958, new regulations for the Alpine Rally permitted the use of larger engines. Taking advantage of this flexibility, Standard-Triumph entered a team of cars fitted with engines incorporating liners to provide a 86mm bore, giving a total swept capacity of 2138cc. This engine was then made available as an option in the TR3A and became the standard power plant later in the TR4 and 4A.

Triumph TR3A – Revised Specification

As TR3 except as noted below:

Engine
Optional 2138cc available from 1959
Bore and stroke 86mm x 92mm
Compression ratio 9.0:1
Max. power 100bhp @ 4,600rpm
Max. torque 127lb ft @ 3,350rpm

Brakes
Size 11 inch diameter discs at front, 10 x 2.25 inch drums at rear
From commission no. TS56377, modified to 9 x 1.75 inch rear drums

Triumph T.R.3 Sports

Ending an era of drawn images and paintings to illustrate the publicity material, the TR3A brochure shows the car in its natural surroundings of a motor-racing circuit.

© BMIHT

FINANCES TAKE A DIP

Towards the end of the 1950s, Standard-Triumph were considering a new model of sports car, rather than a further revision of the side-screen car. A series of situations had arisen that in some ways might have brought back memories of the late 1930s. Standard-Triumph had disposed of its interest in tractor manufacturing and had spent the cash on buying up strategically important component suppliers and, significantly, Mulliners in 1958. In retrospect, this may have seemed an unnecessary expense, but Standard-Triumph were faced with a situation in which the previously independent pressing houses were being

acquired by competitor motor manufacturers. Ford had acquired Briggs Motor Bodies and BMC held control over Fisher and Ludlow; Pressed Steel, which remained independent, was a significant supplier to BMC and the Rootes Group and would in due course merge to form Pressed Steel Fisher. In this environment, Standard-Triumph clearly needed to make moves to ensure continuity and security of pressing facilities.

In a different segment of the market, the Standard 8 and 10 models had given way to the new Herald and a new assembly plant had been built at Canley. The introduction of the Herald was not without its problems and, to compound matters, styles were changing in the United States, the largest market for TRs, with a desire for more creature comforts. Then, to make matters worse, the British government of the time, concerned about the overheating economy, implemented tighter controls over consumer credit. The policy had an immediate and devastating effect on the motor industry. As a precursor to a situation that was to plague the motor industry for the next thirty years, production was rapidly reduced to allow unsold stock to be sold. Not for the first time in its history, the situation facing the Triumph name

looked perilous and plans to introduce a successor car to the side-screen TR were surely at risk.

That might well have been the end of Triumph again had it not been for the ambitions of Leyland Motors Limited, a large and highly successful bus and lorry manufacturer from Lancashire. Leyland had an interest in expanding its business into motor cars and Standard-Triumph were a good fit. As is usual in such business takeovers significant changes were implemented, firm cost controls were put in place and

Leyland Motors Ltd were always more closely associated in the public perception with lorries and buses – it was their success in these markets worldwide that generated the cash necessary to acquire Standard-Triumph.

future model plans were closely analysed. In today's world, the Leyland name has been badly tarnished by association with the much later British Leyland operations. However, at the time of the Standard-Triumph acquisition, Leyland was a highly regarded, cash-rich and profitable business, fulfilling the requirements of many bus operators and haulage businesses, not just in Great Britain, but globally.

After very close scrutiny, the model plans for the TR product range were approved. But there was to be a final appearance for the side-screen car, using substantial components from the car yet to be announced.

THE SIDE SCREEN SWANSONG

Volume motor manufacturers work to a mantra of 'we sell what we build' while the bespoke market follows the ethos of 'we build what we can sell'. Standard-Triumph clearly fell into that first category, but did listen to their dealer network. With the introduction of the TR4 a significant number of dealers, particularly in the United States, considered that the new design and price increase might have a negative impact on

The most distinctive feature of the TR Beta was the new front grille. Although in reality a TR3A, this car has been built as a replica of, or 'tribute' to, the prototype 'Beta' car.

Both Beta prototypes are believed to have survived; this one is undergoing restoration by marque specialist Neil Revington.

A comparison of the front wing of a TR Beta and a TR2 – the additional 2 inches let into each wing to achieve the extra width are quite apparent.

the success of their business and put pressure on Standard-Triumph to retain the earlier side-screen car. The proposed solution was to introduce the new model, but to continue to sell a TR3 car alongside. It was a difficult situation, but a mildly modified version of the side-screen car continued to be made available, for the United States market only. This car became known as the TR3B. Two sets of commission numbers were issued and, to complicate matters slightly, TR3Bs had two distinct specifications: the first 500 cars to be built were fitted with the 1991cc engine, while the remainder of the 3,331 cars built were fitted with the 2138cc engine, the standard fitting in the new TR4. All TR3Bs used the new all-synchromesh gearbox.

As it turned out, the dealers who had questioned the market viability of the new car were proved to be wrong.

A different approach had been considered, using the new TR4-style chassis and running gear, but fitted with a side-screen body. This design was given the name 'Beta'. Because the new chassis was wider than its predecessor, it was necessary to subtly reshape the car to cover the wheels and a revised front grille was used, with the front sidelights and indicators repositioned on to the wings. Two

prototype cars were produced, but the model was not put into production.

Side screen car production ended in 1962, nine years after the first TR sports car had been built and after something in excess of 83,500 cars had been built. More importantly, Triumph was established as a manufacturer of sports cars and that cachet rubbed off on to its entire product range, a benefit that was to continue until the end of production of the Triumph marque.

TRIUMPH TR: HOME-MARKET LIST PRICES FROM BEGINNING TO END

1953	£555	Initial launch price
January 1954	£595	Volume production commences
October 1954	£625	'Short-door' TR2 introduced
October 1955	£680	TR2 evolves into TR3
January 1958	£699	TR3 becomes TR3A

CHAPTER FOUR

TR SPORTING ACHIEVEMENTS

Clubmen immediately take the new TR to their heart, with the car becoming the choice of many to compete in both domestic and international events. Following on from the publicity gained from the Jabbeke speed record, cars compete at Le Mans, showing the robustness and reliability of the design, and in rallying where the inherent strength of the car is used to advantage

EARLY SUCCESSES

Almost as soon as the TR2 went on sale, motorsport success was achieved. Entry into motorsport in the early 1950s was a simple affair. It was quite normal for everyday cars to be driven to events, to compete and, hopefully, to be driven home again, even at the highest level. Preparation was little more than a few extra lamps for night-time rally events, a considered tuning of the engine and perhaps some carefully chosen after-market tuning kits. TR2s had great appeal for the club member and the first competitive success was achieved in January 1954 when car dealer and enthusiastic rally driver Dennis Done achieved victory in Liverpool Motor Club's New Year Rally. Success followed in the RAC Rally of the same year with TR2s entered by John Wallwork, another motor dealer, and Peter Cooper taking first and second place overall as well as winning the 1600cc–2600cc sports car class. Mary Walker won a Coupe des Dames to add to the award tally for the Triumph. The results were summarized in the April 1954 issue of *Motor Sport* as 'A triumph for the TR2 sports car', with a picture of Wallwork's car bearing the registration GJA 205 adorning the front cover. Following on from the record-setting speed test at Jabekke, it was inevitable that Standard-Triumph would embark on a programme of motorsport competition.

Ken Richardson was given the task of managing all of Standard-Triumph's competition entries. From the end of his initial work on the development of the TR until 1961, he managed the Competition Department, overseeing notable works entry successes in Alpine rallying and at Le Mans. The first works entry came in May 1954, in the twenty-first Mille Miglia event in Italy, with three cars being entered. The car driven by the team of Maurice Gatsonides and Ken Richardson achieved a creditable twenty-seventh place overall and tenth in class.

Although *Motor Sport* described the Triumph entry as 'looking rather lost' among the other entries in this class, the TR did exceptionally well for such a new car in its first full year of motorsport. It also achieved good results in the Lyons–Charbonnières rally, with a top-ten placing for a works car borrowed and driven by the then editor of *Autosport*, Gregor Grant. A significant victory was gained by the Triumph works team in the 1954 Rallye des Alpes, captured on film by Standard-Triumph's own publicity unit, with a three-car team again being entered. TR2s finished in 2nd, 3rd and 4th places in the 2000cc class, Triumph won the manufacturers' team prize and the pairing of Gatsonides and Slotemaker was awarded a 'Coupe des Alpes' for a penalty-free finish. The rally was recognized as one of the toughest, a severe test of both cars and competitors, with a route that extended to over 2,200 miles (3,500km).

August 1955 saw both Ken Richardson and Maurice Gatsonides competing in the Liège–Rome–Liège Rally, an event held over four days and nights that placed enormous demands on both car and crew. Richardson finished fifth and Gatsonides seventh.

Relaxing outside the Gray d'Albion hotel in Cannes after winning the Team Prize in the 1954 Alpine Rally, with team manager Ken Richardson on the left. Gatsonides had achieved a 'Coupe des Alpes' driving PDU 20, a car that survives to this day.

© BMIHT

TRIUMPH ON THE CIRCUIT

TRs were winning not just on rallies, but also in circuit racing in 1954, with notable success at the Tourist Trophy meeting held at Dundrod, Northern Ireland. In the production car category, TR2s took five of the top seven places, winning the team prize in the process. For Le Mans in 1954, a single TR2 was entered privately by Edgar Wadsworth, with Bobby Dickson or John Brown as co-driver, achieving fifteenth place. (There is some uncertainty over who was actually the second crew member. The Auto Club de l'Ouest's race data mention Dickson, but the contemporary race report in *Motor Sport* names Brown. Further correspondence does not clarify the matter, with both men being named adamantly as team member.)

For 1955, the most significant event for Triumph was the 24 Hours at Le Mans, captured on film by many amateurs and professionals alike. The Standard Motor Company once again sent its film unit under the direction of Frank Callaby to make a promotional publicity film, with commentary by Raymond Baxter.

Triumph achieved a remarkable overall result for what was a team of effectively road-going cars. Three cars were entered, registered PKV 374, PKV 375 and PKV 376, and all three cars completed the event. However, the 1955 Le Mans was to prove to be an event that would live in the memory of all who witnessed it for other reasons.

At 6:26 pm, at the end of the thirty-fifth lap of racing, the worst accident in the history of motor racing, before or since, occurred, with devastating consequences. The

A TR2 captured at the inaugural Easter Revival held at the Thruxton circuit. TRs remain popular today as classic race cars.

LE MANS 1955 RESULTS

Entry number	Registration	Drivers	Overall position
68	PKV 374	Mortimer Morris-Goodall, Leslie Brooke	19th
29	PKV 375	Ken Richardson, Bert Hadley	15th
28	PKV 376	Bobby Dickson, Ninian Sanderson	14th

Jaguar pit crew signalled Mike Hawthorn to stop his car for refuelling. Hawthorn had just passed an Austin-Healey 100 driven by Lance Macklin and was in front of him when he braked for his pit stop. Macklin was forced to brake hard and swerved across the track to avoid a collision. The Jaguar, like the Triumph TR2s, was fitted with disc brakes and was therefore able to slow significantly faster than the drum-braked Healey. As Macklin swerved, his car moved into the path of a Mercedes 300SLR driven by Pierre Levegh, which was travelling at much higher speed. The Mercedes mounted the rear of Macklin's car and flew across the track before coming into contact with a bank at the edge, where it somersaulted and disintegrated. Heavy objects such as the engine and transmission components flew into the crowd. The fuel tank ruptured, bursting into flames, and the ensuing inferno reached a temperature in excess of that required to ignite the lightweight magnesium alloy of the bodywork. Official figures quote 84 fatalities and 120 injuries. Unofficial figures place the numbers much higher.

The organizers made the decision to continue racing, perhaps considering that an abandonment would cause more difficulties to the rescuers by crowding and blocking of access roads as the spectators left the area. The drivers were forced to witness a harrowing sight each time they passed the pits.

Shortly afterwards, car 68 with Leslie Brooke at the wheel was involved in an incident at Tertre Rouge, the high-speed, ninety-degree right-hand bend immediately preceding the long Mulsanne straight. Overshooting the corner, Brooke's

Looking remarkably like one of the 1955 works Le Mans team cars, PKV 693 was built as a rally car for 1955 and competed in the Tulip Rally of that year. Now used as a classic race car, it is seen here at Goodwood during the 72nd Members' Meeting and has previously competed at Classic Le Mans.

car embedded itself deep into the sand bank and, despite attempts to rock it out with a forward and reverse motion, became stuck fast. The only option was to dig the car out, using a shovel that fortuitously was found close to the corner. Of course, no assistance could be given and the driver was required to dig out his own car.

At 2 am, the Mercedes team was withdrawn. All three Triumphs continued to run well and without incident, barring a small engine fire during a pit stop when oil was dripped on to a hot manifold, but was brought swiftly under control. In an event dominated by teams with far greater resources and larger budgets than Triumph, with cars specially prepared for the event, for the entire Triumph team to complete the event in cars that, essentially, the spectator could go out and purchase the next day was indeed a triumph.

The 1955 Le Mans cars were not absolutely customer standard cars, but the modifications, other than the long-range fuel tanks fitted for the event, were ones that would be available as standard before long. In any case, the cars were being run as prototypes. The engines were fitted with the new high-port cylinder head and all three cars had experimental disc brakes. Two types of disc brakes were used: the four-wheel Dunlop

system was fitted to PKV 376 and the remaining cars were fitted with the Girling disc brake to the front axle and Alfin drums to the rear. It was, of course, the Girling system that was to become a standard fit shortly afterwards on the TR3.

TR3 DOMINATES THE RALLY SCENE

Ken Richardson organized a new set of TR3 cars for the 1956 rally season but these were not to participate in the Monte Carlo Rally for that year. As in 1955, the Monte was campaigned by a mixture of the newly introduced Series III Vanguards and smaller Standard 10 cars, all bearing the Standard badge. The TRs were to achieve an outstanding series of victories in the Alpine Rally in 1956. Once again, Frank Callaby and his film crew accompanied the Competition Department, with Raymond Baxter providing commentary to record what was perhaps Standard-Triumph's best victory. As well as providing the post-production commentary to the film, Baxter also competed in the event driving a Sunbeam Rapier, although he was forced to retire due to accident damage. Overall, seven Triumphs were entered; six were to finish. The only car not to finish was that of Ken Richardson, which was withdrawn from the event after suffering transmission troubles.

A works TR3 driven by the formidable team of Maurice Gatsonides and Ed Pennybacker came home in eighth overall position; the highest-placed Triumph and winner of the 1600cc–2000cc class. Not far behind, Paddy Hopkirk and Willy Cave took overall 13th place and 2nd in class, immediately followed by the Kat brothers, Hans and Philip. Leslie Griffiths and Norman Blockley were in 16th position, with Tommy and Ann Wisdom following, meaning that Triumph took a clean sweep of the top five positions in the class. To round off the awards, a Standard 10 took first place in the up to 1000cc class to add to the silverware to be transported home to Coventry.

Alpine Cups, or 'Coupes des Alpes', were awarded to entrants who achieved a penalty-free completion. All the Triumphs that finished did so without penalties being awarded and were thus awarded with Alpine Cups. In summary, Triumph achieved 1st, 2nd and 3rd in class, the team prize and five Coupes des Alpes. No wonder Raymond Baxter ended his commentary with the phrase, 'Triumph in the Alps'.

For 1957, the success continued, starting with victory in March at Sebring, Florida, in the 12 Hours endurance race. Triumph TR3s finished in 19th and 21st places overall to claim 1st and 2nd positions in the Sports 2000 class. Back in Europe, the rally successes continued with a class win in the Tulip Rally, a team prize in the Liège–Rome–Liège rally, and an award of the Coupe des Dames to Annie Soisbault in the Tour de France.

In 1958, a new set of TR3A team cars, painted in light green, soon began to acquire trophies. A class win for Gatsonides in the Monte Carlo, finishing 6th overall, was followed by a 5th place finish in the gruelling Liège–Rome–Liège rally. Paddy Hopkirk was victorious in the Circuit of Ireland, with Desmond Titterington close behind taking second place. There were class wins in the Tulip Rally and Rally des Alpes and the Coupe des Dames for Annie Soisbault again in the Tour de France.

As the 1950s drew to a close, Triumph prepared another fleet of cars, painted signal red and registered in the WVC

Seen here at Goodwood, SRW 992 was famously driven by veteran driver and journalist Tommy Wisdom, with his daughter Ann as co-driver, in the 1956 Rallye des Alpes. Later it was to achieve fame at Sebring in the 1957 12 Hours race.

MAURICE GATSONIDES: AIRLINE PILOT, RALLY DRIVER, INDUSTRIALIST, NEMESIS OF THE SPEEDING MOTORIST

Born in 1911 in Gombong in Java, where his father was serving in the Royal Dutch diplomatic service, Maurice Gatsonides commenced his career by training as an airline pilot with KLM Royal Dutch Airlines. In 1935, he resigned to set up his own business in the motor trade, based in Haarlem. He began a long association with British motor manufacturers, and particularly those based in Coventry, in 1936 when he drove a Hillman Minx in the Monte Carlo Rally. With the outbreak of the Second World War in 1939, Gatsonides turned his business skills to manufacturing charcoal gas generators to allow petrol-engined vehicles to continue to operate despite the complete removal of petrol from the market. With the end of hostilities in 1945, 'Gatso' built his own car, based on Ford components, using his nickname as a brand. This was a short-lived venture, not helped by the difficulty in sourcing the component parts, but an agency for brands within the Rootes Brothers empire was more lucrative.

His sporting career with Triumph is well documented. As his driving career came to an end, he turned his engineering skills to developing a device to measure his car's speed with the aim of improving its cornering performance. It comprised two rubber strips laid across the road at a pre-determined distance operating 'start' and 'stop' switches on a timing mechanism, allowing the speed of a crossing vehicle to be accurately and irrefutably determined, and was subsequently developed into the system widely used by police forces to enforce speed limits. Later developments gave rise to the 'Gatso' camera, now extensively used for traffic law enforcement. Maurice Gatsonides died in November 1998.

series, WVC 247 to WVC 251. Again, the team racked up the victories, with class wins in the Tulip Rally, the Rallye des Alpes and the team prize in the RAC Rally. By now, however, the TR was beginning to be outpowered by its rival, the Austin Healey. BMC's works department was spending heavily on preparations, but the Triumph, a car that was not specially prepared for competition and remained essentially the same car as the one that could be purchased for road use, continued to perform well in its class, as the record of achievements bears witness.

In the 1958 Alpine Rally, Desmond Titterington drove this works TR3A to take third place in its class and eighth overall.
© BMIHT

'WIN ON SUNDAY, SELL ON MONDAY'

Car manufacturers have always taken advantage of sporting success to enhance their opportunities to sell production cars to the customer. 'Win on Sunday, Sell on Monday' is a phrase often associated with the Ford Motor Company, but the concept of sporting success being used as a marketing tool was well understood by Triumph. Competition achievements were listed on the rear cover of the sales brochures leaving the prospective buyer in no doubt that this was a car with a sporting pedigree:

TR2 Brochure:

BELGIUM
1953	Jabbeke Highway, 124mph in speed trim

IRELAND
1954	21st RAC International TT Team Award
1955	Circuit of Ireland Trial: 1st, 2nd and 3rd and Team Award

ALPINE RALLY
1954	Team Award 2000cc class, 2nd, 3rd and 4th

USA
1954	Lockbourne Races, Ohio, 1st, 2nd and 3rd in 150-mile race, 1st, 2nd and 3rd in 50-mile race

SOUTH AMERICA
1954	El Autodromo de Maracay, Venezuela, Sports Cars up to 2600cc, 1st; Gran Premion Alcadia de Bogota, Columbia, 1st and 2nd, General Classification, 2nd; High Speed Race, Guatemala City, 1st

UNITED KINGDOM
1954	RAC Rally, General Classification, 1st and 2nd; Sports Car Class, 1st, 2nd and 3rd; Ladies Award; Team Award, 2nd and 3rd
1955	RAC Rally, Sports Car Class, 1st, General Classification, 2nd

FRANCE
1954	Le Mans 24 Hours. Competing against International-type racing cars, the privately entered TR2 averaged 74.71mph for 24 hours with a petrol consumption of 34.7 miles to the gallon
1955	Le Mans 24 Hours. A works team of three TR2s all completed the course, the two leaders averaging almost 85mph for the 24 hours

CHINA
1954	Grand Prix of Macau, 1st, 2nd and 3rd

The TR3 brochure included the same information but added the following:

BELGIUM
1956	Les Douze Heures de Nivelles 2000cc Class, 1st and 2nd

IRELAND
1956	Circuit of Ireland Trial, 1st, 2nd and 3rd

ALPINE RALLY
1956	Team Award; 2000cc Class, 1st, 2nd, 3rd, 4th and 5th. 5 Alpine Cups

GERMANY
1956	Rally Trifels, 2000cc Class, 1st, 2nd and 3rd

Finally, for the 1958 TR3A brochure, the list grew even longer, with some earlier successes in the United States added for good measure:

ALPINE RALLY
1958	1600cc, unlimited class, 1st and 2nd

LIÈGE–ROME– LIÈGE
1957	1300cc–2000cc Class, 2nd, 3rd and 5th; manufacturers' team prize; General Classification, 3rd, 5th and 9th
1958	1601cc–2000cc class, 1st

continued overleaf

'WIN ON SUNDAY, SELL ON MONDAY' *continued*

TULIP RALLY		USA	
1958	Normal Grand Touring Production	1954	Torrey Pines, stock over 1500cc,
	Cars 1600cc–2000cc, 1st and 3rd		1st, 2nd and 3rd in class; 3rd overall,
IRELAND			all classes over 1500cc; Race 14,
1958	Circuit of Ireland Trial, 1st, 2nd, 3rd,		all classes over 1500cc, 1st in class,
	5th, 6th, 7th		3rd overall
FRANCE		1955	Pebble Beach, Cypress Point
1957	Tour de France, Coupe des		Handicap, 1st, 2nd and 3rd in class.
	Dames		5th overall, 3rd in class, Main Event
1957	Rally of Corsica, Ladies Prize; 1st in	1957	National, Elkhart Lake, 1st in class
	class, general classification		

BACK TO LE MANS

Despite the terrible tragedy of the 1955 event, the 24 Hours went ahead in 1956, following modifications to the circuit in the pit area. Both the 1956 and 1957 events took place with no Triumph interest, but in 1958, although no actual Triumph cars were entered, a Peerless GT driven by Peter Jopp and Percy Crab and powered by a Triumph engine did compete. The Peerless GT (see Chapter 10), was a limited production car built around TR3 sub-assemblies. With the encouragement and support of the Standard-Triumph board, including assistance with preparing the car, a single car was entered, with a second in reserve. The cars were newly introduced to the market and only lightly modified. It was perhaps with some surprise that in typical Le Mans wet weather the car not only finished the event in sixteenth place overall, but also finished as winner of the 2-litre class.

The second half of the 1950s saw a growth of interest in double overhead cam designs. Jaguar had established their XK engines on the track, particularly at Le Mans, and the MGA was available with a double overhead cam engine, although this was not without problems, leading to a rather brief life. The Jaguar engine was highly successful and enjoyed a long production life, from its initial introduction in 1949 until the end of production in 1992. Somewhat ironically, it was developed as a replacement for the Standard engines fitted in what were known as 'SS' cars prior to the renaming as 'Jaguar', following the Second World War. In Grand Prix

racing, Coventry Climax were also achieving success with double overhead cam designs so it was hardly surprising that Triumph should look at the technology to supplant the wet-liner engine that had powered the TR through the 1950s. In fact, as events were subsequently to unfold, it would do so until the introduction of the TR5.

Motorsport provides a perfect environment for development and in 1958, the decision was made to return to Le Mans for the 1959 competition. At a distance, the cars to be entered appeared to be TR3As, but they were actually 6 inches (150mm) longer in the wheelbase and were fitted with glass-fibre body panels. The most significant change could be seen under the bonnet, where the familiar overhead valve engine had been replaced with something far more exotic. That extra length had been added to accommodate the installation of the new engine. Officially designated as 20X, the new engine immediately became known as the 'Sabrina' – presumably because the covers fitted over the cylinder head timing gear bore a resemblance to the prominent features of the British starlet of that name! The official designation of the cars was TR3S.

The engine was a completely new design, taking advantage of lightweight alloy castings for all major assemblies except for the crankcase, which was cast from iron. Fuel supply was by way of dual twin-choke SU carburettors and the engine developed 150bhp at 6,500rpm. Although this new engine design was never to be used in production cars, care was taken in the design to ensure that it had the potential to be

THE 'OTHER' SABRINA

Born in Stockport, Cheshire, in May 1936, Norma Ann Sykes became a glamour model of the 1950s under the stage name of 'Sabrina'. Her hour-glass figure, much in vogue at the time, placed her in the same company as Marilyn Monroe, Jayne Mansfield and Diana Dors. Aged nineteen, she appeared on television alongside Arthur Askey in the TV series *Before Your Very Eyes* from 1952 to 1958 in a non-speaking role. She was also cast in various British film productions of the era. In those less politically correct days, her physical attributes were the key to her fame and her stage name was often used as a descriptor both in and beyond the motor industry.

mass-produced in limited quantities; some consideration had been given to the creation of a top-of-the-range TR using the Le Mans engine. This was not to be Triumph's first twin overhead cam engine; the 8-cylinder engine fitted to the 1930s Dolomite 8C had been similarly equipped.

Three cars were entered for the 1959 24 Hours at Le Mans, registered XHP 938, XHP 939 and XHP 940, and the press and public got their first sight of the new cars during testing in April 1959 prior to the event. The cars were built on a chassis that was essentially that of a production TR3A, with necessary allowances for the new engine, fitted with disc brakes on all wheels and with strengthening added to the chassis side members. Despite the use of fibreglass for the body panels, these were no lightweight race cars. Each car weighed almost a ton. Fibreglass construction was a new technique at Standard-Triumph and the panels had been made thicker than necessary, which added considerable weight. It was questionable whether the additional chassis strengthening was even necessary on such a smooth circuit. Perhaps Triumph were influenced by their experience in rallying? Unusually for cars entered for Le Mans, cooling fans had been fitted to each car's engine and this was to prove to be the Achilles heel for two of the cars.

LE MANS 1959; SUCCESS OR FAILURE?

First to retire after thirty-five laps and four hours of running was the car crewed by Peter Bolton and Michael Rothschild, followed about six hours later by Peter Jopp and Richard 'Dickie' Stoop. Both cars had suffered from the same problem: the cooling fan had pierced the radiator, with inevitable results. To prevent this happening on the third car, driven by Ninian Sanderson and Claude Dubois, a pit-stop modification was made with the removal of the fan blades. Sadly, this car also failed to finish; in the twenty-third hour of the event, it was forced to withdraw following a failure of the engine oil pump. At the time, the car was in seventh place overall and leading in its class. Later analysis showed that the engine mounts had softened during racing and, under the extreme braking conditions of the Sarthe circuit, the engine had been able to move forwards enough for the spinning fan blades to make contact with the radiator.

The cars were returned to Coventry and taken apart, with the running gear becoming the basis of the new cars that would race at Le Mans in 1960. The official record showed that the bodies of all three cars were destroyed, but rumours persisted for many years that one body had escaped destruction. It is now generally accepted that one of the bodies, or at least parts of it, have survived.

TR3S BECOMES TRS

For the 1960 event, Triumph created four new cars using the modified underpinnings of the TR3S cars. The track was wider, as would be the case for the yet to be launched TR4, and rack and pinion steering was fitted. The body style exhibited certain similarities with a design study that had been under consideration as a replacement style for the side-screen cars and was constructed of glass-fibre. Again, the cars were heavy, even more so than the TR3Ss of the previous year, and suffered from poor aerodynamics, resulting in lap times of ten seconds slower than the cars in 1959.

Four cars made the journey to Le Mans; three were to race and the fourth car was available to be cannibalized as a

TRS OR TR4S?

With the earlier cars being designated TR3S, it might be assumed that the Le Mans cars that were to follow would be designated TR4S. This mistake has been compounded by certain online resources inaccurately designating the cars as such. At the time, the TR4 car was still a future product and by 1961, the body design differed in many respects from that of the cars raced at Le Mans, so there was no reason why the TR4 reference should have been used. This can be confirmed by reference to contemporary magazine reports on the races, which refer to the cars (correctly) as TRS, by anecdotal evidence from those who worked with and on the cars, and from those who attended the event in 1960 or 1961 as spectators.

The TRS cars at Le Mans during the 1960 event.
© BMIHT

source of parts if required. The three cars entered into the event ran reliably, finishing in 15th, 18th and 19th place overall and in their class, beaten only by a twin-cam MGA. The event for Peter Bolton very nearly came to a premature end as his car appeared to stall while pulling away from the traditional Le Mans start. Luckily, he was able to restart the car and continue.

Sadly, none of the cars could be classified, because they all failed to achieve the minimum distance specified. During the event, all were losing power caused by valve clearances closing up as a result of the valve seats receding. More work was going to be required for the 1961 event.

LE MANS 1960

Registration	Entry number	Crew	Finishing position
926 HP	28	Keith Ballisat/Marcel Becquart	15th
927 HP	29	Peter Bolton/Ninian Sanderson	19th
928 HP	59	Les Leston/Mike Rothschild	18th

TRIUMPH AGAIN

After the disappointment of failing to complete the required distance in 1960, the problems with the valves were fully investigated and modifications made. For the 1961 event, three of the four TRS cars were taken to Le Mans and this time all three not only finished the event but also covered sufficient distance for the results to count. 926 HP ran without any problems throughout the entire twenty-four hours; 927 suffered ignition problems caused by a faulty coil in the early stages of the race and 929 HP – the car which had been spare in the 1960 event – suffered a failed oil seal and finished only after temporary repairs had been undertaken. The three cars achieved 9th, 11th and 15th position overall, results that were good enough to win for Triumph the coveted manufacturers' team prize.

All three 1961 cars were retired after Le Mans and sold via the dealer network in North America where they all survive in the care of enthusiasts.

This was not to be quite the end of the TRS cars at Le Mans – a final car based loosely on the TRS formula would be built, but never raced. While gifted Italian designer Giovanni Michelotti was finding favour within Standard-Triumph (see also Chapter 5), fellow Italian Virgilio Conrero was establishing a reputation for the development of engines and suspension, achieving significant success with tuned Alfa-Romeo models. With both Michelotti and Vignale having a working relationship with Triumph, it was inevitable that Conrero's abilities would come to the notice of the British company and it was to Conrero that Triumph turned to develop the next generation of Le Mans race cars. In parallel with preparations for the 1961 event, a totally different design was envisaged. It was perhaps unfortunate that Standard-Triumph was at the time on the brink of bankruptcy once again, but a single car was to be completed based on TR running gear, with a Sabrina engine, two twin-choke Weber carburettors and a fixed-head coupé body designed by Michelotti. The completed car was lighter than the

TRS cars and, with a more streamlined body and, therefore, an improved drag coefficient, it would probably have performed better than the TRS cars. However, with the Competitions Department being closed soon after the 1961 Le Mans event, the opportunity to prove the car never arose. It was registered as 3097 KV and was exported to the United States.

Triumph were to return to Le Mans with works cars in the future, but this would be with the Spitfire, competing in a different class. As it turned out, the team prize success of 1961 would mark the conclusion of the story of TR works entries.

LE MANS 1961

Registration	Entry number	Crew	Finishing position
926 HP	27	Keith Ballisat/Peter Bolton	9th
927 HP	26	Les Leston/Rob Slotemaker	11th
929 HP	25	Marcel Becquart/Mike Rothschild	15th

Twin SU carburettors are nothing unusual but twin-choke SUs are something quite different. They were fitted by Triumph to the 'Sabrina' engines in twin configuration, effectively giving a carburettor per cylinder.

CHAPTER FIVE

THE MICHELOTTI CARS

As the 1960s loom, Triumph perceives the market moving from a simple and rugged low-slung car into something with a little more creature comfort. A chance introduction to Giovanni Michelotti provides Triumph with a stunning range of cars ideally suited to the new decade. Outstanding among these is the new TR4. Much as the Belgrove-styled side-screen car had epitomized Triumph style during the 1950s, Michelotti's design sees Triumph through the 1960s.

The original side-screen TR continued to sell in significant numbers through the late 1950s, but Standard-Triumph could not ignore the need for a successor car to be even better if it was to succeed in the marketplace, both at home and, more importantly, in the United States. In the USA, the concept of the annual model design change had become well established and, by the time the last TR3B finally left production, its design had remained fundamentally unchanged since 1953. Despite the market-leading innovations seen with the TR, the competition was catching up: MG were now selling the MGA in quantity and Healey's 'Big' model, still being built by Austin, had by the late 1950s grown both in dimensions and engine capacity.

From 1956 onwards, Standard-Triumph faced a series of difficulties with design and styling. Long-time Chief Body Engineer Walter Belgrove had left the company and his former department was without leadership just as work was required to develop a replacement for the little Standard 8 and 10 models, as well as the evolution of the TR. Vic Hammond, who had worked in Belgrove's department, was charged with developing a replacement for the TR3. By the spring of 1957, this had evolved into a design that might well have become the definitive Triumph TR4 had a chance meeting not steered the direction elsewhere.

THE ITALIAN JOB

Raymond Flower was a Midlands businessman with family connections to the Stratford-on-Avon brewers, a distribu-

tor of BMC vehicles in Egypt and the man behind the Frisky microcar. At a meeting with Harry Webster and Martin Tustin at Standard-Triumph, in connection with a completely unrelated project, Flower drew their attention to a talented designer working in Turin, Italy. Webster and Tustin were particularly interested in Flower's claim that his contact could design and build fully painted and trimmed prototype cars in a time scale of around two months. By way of a challenge, Flower was asked to forward a request to Italy for the design of a sports car that was required urgently. Within two weeks, a series of design sketches were provided, along with a price quotation for the full design work to be undertaken. The cost estimate was far below the equivalent for a similar design concept to be developed in the United Kingdom. A TR3 rolling chassis was soon shipped to Turin for the design to be developed. Within three months, the work was completed and Tustin and Webster were able to visit Italy to view the result and to be introduced to the designer, Giovanni Michelotti. Webster is quoted as saying, 'It didn't take me long to decide that we really ought to sign him up for our future work' (*Triumph TRs – The Complete Story*, Robson, G.).

The prototype design soon picked up the name 'dream car'. It was shipped to Coventry and placed alongside Hammond's design for management approval. Engineers from Mulliners were invited to provide a production costing for the design, but their report was not to the management's liking. Features such as rear fins, hooded headlights and wind-up windows added significantly to the tooling cost and the

An early example of the TR4, dating from 1962, showing the unmistakable Michelotti style. After-market seats are fitted – the giveaway is the headrests, which were not an option on a TR until very much later.

Michelotti's first TR design for Triumph was a very futuristic design that did not meet with full approval, not least because of the cost of production.

decision was made not to proceed with the design. However, it did result in a long-term contract between Standard-Triumph and Michelotti. His first formal task for the company was what would today be called a 'facelift' of the Standard Vanguard, followed by the styling of the car, code-named 'Zobo', that was to replace the Standard 8 and 10 and would be launched in 1959 as the Triumph Herald. The next project was to be the development of a new style for the TR4.

DESIGN CHANGES AND Z CARS

Both Hammond's and Michelotti's original proposals had been designed around the locating points of the TR3 chassis, but it took some time for the exact chassis dimensions to be confirmed. Thought was given to widening the wheel track, to lengthening the wheelbase and to providing the mountings to allow the Sabrina twin overhead cam engine developed for the Le Mans race cars to be installed in a range-topping model. Like most manufacturing concerns, Standard-Triumph used a series of code names to describe products in development at this period; future cars were given a four-letter word beginning with a 'Z' as the code name.

Michelotti developed numerous concepts based on various wheelbase and track combinations, of which 'Zest' was the first, built on an unmodified TR3A chassis. Some of the key design points of the TR4 become apparent in Zest, including the hooded headlights and the 'shoulder' curve situated at the rear of the doors that was to become a feature of all future separate chassis Triumph sports cars. Zest also featured a hard top, borrowed from the roof style developed for the Herald Coupé. 'Zoom' was another design study on a long wheelbase and wide-track chassis. The side profile was similar to that of Zest, but the front view pre-dated the design that was to be used on the future Triumph Spitfire and, much later, the TR6. In between all these design exercises, Michelotti penned an elegant fixed-head coupé based on an unmodified TR3A chassis. This car was to go

Early proposals for the new TR4. The design on the left is an in-house study, positioned next to Michelotti's design. In the end, neither design was to be taken forward.

© BMIHT

into production in Italy, built by Vignale on Triumph underpinnings and sold as the Triumph Italia.

Eventually, the chassis configuration was fixed. The wheelbase of the outgoing TR3A was retained, the track was increased by 4 inches (10cm) and rack and pinion steering was to be fitted. Michelotti could now develop the definitive TR4 style, using the general profile of Zoom but incorporating the frontal view from Zest. The long, front-hinged bonnet incorporated a power bulge on the right side as viewed from the cockpit, just off centre, to provide clearance for twin carburettors. This feature was to remain on all Michelotti cars even when it was no longer required for the car that was to follow the TR4.

In terms of creature comforts, the car provided wind-up windows and retained, at least in theory, the option of an occasional rear seat. Weather equipment was now restricted to a hood that was assembled over roof sticks, in the manner of the earlier side-screen cars, with the cover stored in the boot when not in use. This allowed the full space behind the front seats to be used for luggage whether or not the roof was erected. Instrumentation followed the same general layout as on the earlier cars and the handbrake was still of the 'fly-off' type. The dashboard on early cars was in metal, painted white, but later cars were to receive a wooden dashboard, establishing a trademark design feature for all Triumphs. The new TR4 featured a 'first' for a sports car by providing face-level fresh-air ventilation through vents fitted to the extreme edges of the dashboard. The interior design of the car needed little improvement over its lifetime, other than a modification to the seats at the end of 1962.

DONALD STOKES

'The toughest job held by any boss in Britain.' (*Financial Times*)

Donald Gresham Stokes was born in March 1914 in Plymouth, where his father was employed by the City as Traffic Manager. In 1930 at the age of sixteen he began an engineering apprenticeship with the firm of Leyland Motors. He died in July 2008 as Baron Stokes of Leyland.

Other than a break for military service, during which he was with the Corps of Royal Electrical and Mechanical Engineers (REME) and rose to the rank of Lieutenant-Colonel, Stokes was to remain with Leyland and its successors for his entire career. On his return to civilian life, Stokes was able to convince his management that an export drive was critical to drive the business during the austerity period. It was a strategy that was completely aligned with the political thinking of the new Labour Government. Furthermore, Stokes was the right person to lead that drive. A naturally gifted salesman, going to any lengths to secure a deal, Stokes was to lead Leyland to great success in the commercial vehicle market worldwide. Under his guidance, Leyland became a market leader in all road-haulage markets and the primary supplier of chassis for passenger carriage, with both municipal and private bus operators selecting Leyland products as first choice.

Success in this role led inexorably to general management, and Stokes was appointed Managing Director of Leyland Motors in 1963 and consequently became titular head of Standard-Triumph, which was by now a component part of Leyland. Coming to the notice of the Wilson-led Labour Government, Sir Donald Stokes, as he now was, was invited to assist the arms industry in its export efforts, appointed to various offices overseeing and advising on industrial strategy, and ultimately persuaded of the wisdom of merging his company with British Motor Holdings. In theory it was a merger, but in reality it was a reverse takeover. Despite Stokes' past business successes, it was clear that his new position running British Leyland was beyond even his capabilities – indeed, it was probably beyond anyone else at the time.

Raised to the House of Lords as Baron Stokes of Leyland in 1969, he was forced by the economic crisis of the early 1970s to go cap in hand to the newly re-elected Labour Government. As was usual at the time, a report was commissioned, which resulted in the nominal promotion of Stokes to non-executive President, effectively removing him from any direct involvement in the business.

Stokes's legacy lies in his recognizing the strength of the Standard-Triumph brand, rescuing that company from near bankruptcy and driving the model range of the 1960s, including TRs from the TR4, to the end of production.

The occasional rear seat was continued in the TR4, although leg room was a little restricted. The TR3-style roof was continued; when removed, the frame collapsed and was hidden behind upholstered flaps that formed the backrest to the rear seat. The front seats in this car are not original.

Front lighting consisted of separate sidelights and indicators. The headlights remained inset at the very front of the car, but the 'eyebrows' recalled the styling of the earlier TRs.

The bonnet of the car featured a distinctive bulge to provide clearance for the twin carburettors.

Rear view of an early TR4 showing the new chromed bumper fitted with large over-riders and chromed rear-light fittings. Badging was limited to a simple TR4 logo and the manufacturer's name.

Initially fitted with SU HS6 carburettors, Zenith-Stromberg 175CD models became the standard fitting, in common with other cars in the Triumph range. SU carburettors have an enthusiastic following and conversions were popular.

ABOVE LEFT: **A simple pressed-steel painted wheel was supplied as standard, with wire wheels a common and very attractive option on the Michelotti-designed cars. Steel wheels were finished with an attractive large chromed hub cap with the Triumph globe badge at the centre.**

ABOVE RIGHT: **The instruments were very similar to those fitted in the earlier side-screen cars and followed the same layout. The positioning of the switchgear was rearranged and an optional radio could be fitted. The 'fly-off' handbrake was still positioned close to the driver's leg. This car retains its original sprung steering wheel.**

ABOVE LEFT: **The TR4 introduced the concept of eye-level fresh-air ventilation, fitted at the extreme edges of the dashboard. An early example, this car retains its white-painted dashboard.**

ABOVE RIGHT: **Other than the modern inertia safety belts fitted, the cockpit of this TR4 retains its 'as delivered' appearance.**

SURREY TOP – ANOTHER FIRST

Whereas the TR3A could be supplied with an optional hard top, a different approach was taken for the TR4, based on a concept first shown on the Zoom study. Instead of the tra-ditional removable hard top, Michelotti had proposed a new design consisting of a fixed rear glass set into a sheet-metal rear window frame that was semi-permanently fitted to the rear panel between the cockpit and forward of the boot lid. This screen incorporated a severe curve and, with its single-piece glazing, provided both rearward and side-quarter visibility.

On top of this unit, a choice of covers could be fitted. During winter, the owner might chose to fit a metal cover, located at the front on to the windscreen header rail and at the back on to the frame. This provided all the benefits of a conventional hard top and could be easily removed. Its size meant that it could not be stored either inside the car or the boot, so a lightweight frame assembled from metal rods could be fitted across the aperture to be covered with a lightweight vinyl cover. Taking its cue from the traditional horse-drawn carriage, this lightweight cover was referred to as a 'Surrey'.

LEFT: **The new-style hard top for the TR4 later became known as the 'Surrey' top. The rear screen was fitted permanently to the car, but the metal lid could be removed and stored off the car. A lightweight fabric cover could be fitted in case of inclement weather.**

BELOW: **The rear view of the Surrey top shows the good all-round visibility offered by the stylish rear screen.**

ABOVE: **Fitting the Surrey top creates a very attractive side view. This example is a TR4A.**

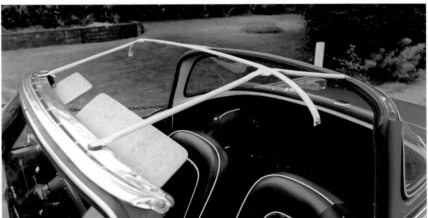

LEFT: **A simple frame allows for the fabric top to be fitted. It can be seen that the hard-top rear window provides for an increase in storage space. It is possible to remove the rear screen and fit a traditional folding roof, but who would want to?**

The same car, this time with the fabric roof fitted.

The Surrey top rapidly became a desirable option on the new TR4 and a highly distinctive feature of the Michelotti cars. It would be a further four years before a similar design concept emerged from Porsche. They called it a 'targa' – a term that was quickly registered as a trademark by Porsche AG.

MECHANICAL CHANGES

The chassis design of the TR4 was an evolution from that used for the TR3A. On first inspection, it looks very similar. To accommodate the wider track, the front of the chassis was widened by the use of extra side members and a wider

Triumph TR4 – Original Specification

Layout and Chassis
Two-seat sports car with separate chassis

Engine

Type	Standard-Triumph 'wet liner'
Block material	Cast iron
Head material	Cast iron
Cylinders	4 in-line
Cooling	Water
Bore and stroke	86mm bore, 92mm stroke (optionally 83mm bore, 92mm stroke)
Capacity	2138cc (optionally 1991cc)
Valves	2 valves per cylinder ohv
Compression ratio	9:1
Carburettor	2 SU HS6, later cars fitted with 2 Zenith-Stromberg 175CDs
Max. power	100bhp @ 4,600rpm (optionally 100bhp @ 4,800rpm)
Max. torque	127lb ft @ 3,350rpm (optionally 117lb ft @ 3,000rpm)
Fuel capacity	11.7 gallons (53.1 litres)

Transmission

Clutch	Single dry plate, hydraulic actuation
Gearbox	S-T 4-speed with synchromesh on all forward speeds
Ratios	
1st	3.14:1
2nd	2.00:1
3rd	1.33:1
4th	1.00:1
Overdrive (optional)	0.82:1
Reverse	3.22:1
Final drive	3.7:1, 4.1:1 when overdrive fitted

Suspension and Steering

Front	Independent using unequal-length wishbones, coil springs and telescopic dampers
Rear	Live axle, half-elliptical leaf springs, lever-arm dampers
Steering	Rack and pinion
Tyres	5.50 or 5.90 – 15 inch crossply
Wheels	Pressed-steel disc wheels with 4-stud fixing. Optional centre-lock wire wheels
Rim width	4 inches

Brakes

Type	Front discs, rear drums
Size	
Front:	10.9 inches diameter
Rear:	9.0 x 1.75 inches

Dimensions

Track	
Front	49 inches (1,245mm)
Rear	48 inches (1,220mm)
Wheelbase	88 inches (2,235mm)
Overall length	154 inches (3,910mm)
Overall width	57.5 inches (1,460mm)
Overall height	50 inches (1,270mm)
Unladen weight	2,240lb (1,015kg)

Performance

Top speed	103mph (165km/h)
0–60mph	10.9 sec

BUILDING THE TR4

Hall Engineering Limited had established a relationship with Triumph for the supply of body components for the Herald model range and particularly for the large complex bonnet, which effectively comprised the front of the car. Despite Hall Engineering's primary business being light metal pressings, notably office furniture, a decision was taken to utilize their facilities to construct the entire body shell for the new TR4. The business was brought into the Standard-Triumph Group in 1960, becoming the Liverpool Number 1 factory. Hall Engineering owned the Dunstable, Bedfordshire business of Auto Body Dies, which provided the press tools needed to create the various body panels.

All this occurred in a very tight time schedule, and against the background of the Leyland Motors takeover. The final design for the car was agreed in the third quarter of 1960, the tools and jigs were completed by the summer of 1961, early production cars left the Canley assembly plant in August of that year and the public launch of the new car took place just one month later. With body shells being constructed in Liverpool and final assembly taking place in Canley, there was a continual convoy of body shells being transported between the two facilities using a fleet of specially designed transporters, each capable of carrying twelve finished body assemblies.

TR4 – THE COMPETITORS

Throughout the 1950s the market for sports cars had been evolving, from the rugged towards the more civilized, with increased creature comforts. The primary competitor for the new TR came from MG, much more so once the new MGB replaced the MGA in the late spring of 1962. The

'Big' Healey, while it might still be considered as a purchase by a prospective owner, was now being sold with a 3-litre 6-cylinder engine and the Sunbeam Alpine had evolved into a car that had visual similarities with Triumph's Zoom design study.

rear axle was of course necessary. The steering column had some provision for its length to be adjusted and a friction joint provided for a small element of safety in the event of an accident – although, by today's standards, this protection was very minimal. In keeping with the practice at the time, 'crash protection' foam was fitted to the top of the dashboard and around the switch panel.

With the overall weight of the car increased over the side-screen cars, the 2138cc engine was the default option, although the 1991cc engine could be specified, most likely to meet the requirements for cars intended for competition. The gearbox was also redesigned to add synchromesh on all forward gears. This general form remained the norm, fitted to all TRs until the introduction of the TR7 much later in the story, as well as the soon-to-be-announced Triumph 2000

saloon and the future Triumph Stag. Overdrive remained a desirable option. Mechanically, the only significant change was a change from twin SU HS6 carburettors to twin Zenith-Stromberg 175CDs in 1963.

TR4 COMPETITORS

	TR4	MGB	Sunbeam Alpine Series II	A-H 3000
Engine capacity	2138cc	1798cc	1592cc	2912cc
0–60mph time	10.9 seconds	11.2 seconds	13.6 seconds	10.9 seconds
Max power	100bhp	95bhp	80bhp	132bhp
Max torque	127lb ft	110lb ft	94lb ft	172lb ft

LEFT: **The MGB replaced the MGA in 1962, just after the introduction of the TR4, and was to stay in production until 1980.**

BELOW: **Frequently referred to as the 'Big' Healey, the Austin-Healey 3000, as it had now become, overlapped production of the TR4. In motorsport, the Healey remained as a formidable competitor against the smaller-engined TR, but in real-life road use, the difference in performance was marginal.**

WHAT DID THE MARKET THINK?

If Triumph were anticipating the same universally positive motoring press reaction to the new TR4 as they had received for the TR2 eight years earlier, they were to be disappointed. Although reviews were generally good, there was one aspect of the new car that attracted criticism.

It began with a report in *Autocar* published in January 1962. The retention of many features from the earlier cars, such as spritely performance and crisp gear change, coupled with well-spaced gears now including synchromesh on all forward gears (a feature that was by no means universal in the early 1960s), was appreciated, but there were comments in some quarters that perhaps the market might be expecting something entirely new. The rack and pinion steering was described as 'exceptionally good', both lightweight in use and precise. The new style was appealing, as was the additional storage space for luggage.

Opinions on the suspension were much less positive. Perhaps the reviewers had been anticipating a new chassis and not the continuation of the side-screen frame? It was reported that 'the ride [was] still decidedly harsh, with the result that the wheels [tended] to hop over any but the smoothest of surfaces'. Particular note was made of the handling on continental pavé surfaces, where bottoming of the rear suspension created quite violent vertical movements in the car. In addition, 'in hard cornering, the rear wheels [would] break away fairly readily'.

Autocar's test car had been a convertible model without overdrive. *Motor* tested a similar car, but theirs was equipped with a Surrey top and overdrive. Their review was similar in theme to that of *Autocar*: there was positive comment in some areas but also severe criticism of the harshness of the rear suspension. According to the tester, 'on well-surfaced main roads the ride [was] flat and unexpectedly comfortable', but '[deteriorated] quickly on second-class surfaces'; the suspension did not 'encourage relaxed cruising at speeds much over 80mph'. (Of course, the publication of these reviews pre-dated the almost universal imposition of speed limits on all roads across Europe.) Some body shake was also mentioned.

At the time of testing, the price for the test car was quoted as £827 10s, with purchase tax bringing the total price to £1,138 16s 6d.

In the United States, *Road & Track* published a test that was more positive and more inclined to praise Triumph, asserting that prospective customers could anticipate a very reliable car that would be enjoyable to drive and offer excellent performance at a moderate initial price. Almost damning with faint praise, the article concluded thus: 'We don't think the improvements are as great as should have been made' but 'Standard-Triumph has a real winner here if production can keep up with demand'.

Clearly, the weak aspect of the new car as far as the 'experts' were concerned was the rear suspension. It so happened that Standard-Triumph had a solution to be introduced, based on the rear suspension design that had been used to great success in the recently introduced Triumph 2000 saloon car.

TR4A – INDEPENDENT REAR SUSPENSION

Successfully retaining all the aspects of the new car that had achieved positive acclaim in the market and with a body design that was still new and attractive, Triumph set about addressing the perceived weakness of the TR4 with a new chassis design. The key requirements of the new chassis were to provide for a softer ride and to increase the rear-wheel movement. Although the front was retained, the centre section was strengthened and the rear was completely new. Building on the semi-trailing arm set-up fitted to the 2000 saloon, the new TR4A for 1965 used the same design of cast trailing arms with coil springs and lever-arm dampers. The dampers were perhaps an anachronism, but space limitations precluded the use of telescopic dampers. (This is a relatively common modification fitted to cars today, using an adaptor kit.) The differential unit was now mounted to the chassis, with the drive being taken through exposed half-shafts fitted with universal joints both inboard and outboard and a splined joint in the drive shaft permitting suspension movement.

In a move reminiscent of the introduction of the original TR4, some members of the US dealer network expressed concern about their ability to sell the independently suspended car. They requested that the existing beam-axle car be retained, especially if the price could be reduced. Well aware of the importance of the US market to sales revenues, Standard-Triumph once again acquiesced, offering a beam-axle TR4A, but only in North America. Simply retaining the earlier design in production alongside the new IRS cars was not an option, however, and the new chassis had to be modified to accommodate the older rear-axle design, with supports for leaf springs being re-fitted.

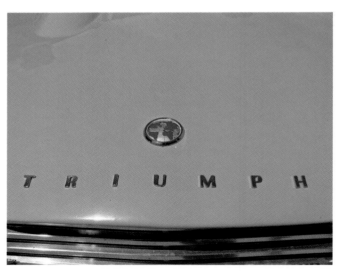

ABOVE: **With the introduction of the TR4A, the bonnet badges changed. The Standard-Triumph shield, which had adorned the front of every TR to date, was replaced with the Triumph globe and the maker's name spelled out underneath.**

LEFT: **The TR4A sales brochure used this illustration to demonstrate the new trailing arm independent rear suspension installation.**
© BMIHT

Perhaps the most attractive British sports car ever built? A TR4A with the desirable Surrey roof and chromed wire wheels, finished in bright red paintwork.

The new model could be easily identified by the additional chromed flash fitted from the repeater lamps to the rear of the doors.

ABOVE LEFT: **With the sidelights now fitted to the wings along with a repeater for the turn signal lamps, the TR4A was fitted with a new, less fussy radiator grille, still incorporating a hole for a starting handle. The over-riders were also reduced in size.**

ABOVE RIGHT: **An interesting detail: the sidelight and turn signal repeater unit that also serves as an ending to the chromed side moulding on the TR4A.**

Body changes were quite subtle. A new bright styling flash was fitted along the swage line from the rear of the door to the front of the wing, which terminated in a new design incorporating side marker lamps and repeater for the turn signal. The side lamps were therefore deleted from the front grille, which was in any case a new design. Bonnet badges were revised: the Triumph lettering was retained, but the Standard-derived shield badge was replaced with a Triumph globe. From the rear, a noticeable feature was twin exhaust pipes, exiting one on each side of the car.

ABOVE LEFT: **Twin exhaust pipes were fitted and remain on this particular car. Over the years, many cars have had revised exhaust systems fitted, with a single pipe emerging from the rear of the car.**

ABOVE RIGHT: **The 4A emphasized its sophistication in the suspension department to following motorists through this badge. It was fitted to the rear of all TR4As, apart from those US models that retained the live axle.**

ABOVE: **The two most obvious differences between a TR4 and 4A cockpit are the repositioning of the handbrake to the transmission tunnel, still of the 'fly-off' variety, and the addition of a wooden dashboard. The steering wheel of this car is not the original fitted at the factory, but a common and very popular after-market addition.**

RIGHT: **Under the bonnet, little had changed from the earliest TR2. This TR4A has been fitted with SU carburettors and an optional remote brake servo, but otherwise retains the appearance of a newly delivered car of 1966.**

Triumph TR4A – Original Specification

Layout and Chassis
Two-seat sports car with separate chassis

Engine

Type	Standard-Triumph 'wet liner'
Block material	Cast iron
Head material	Cast iron
Cylinders	4 in-line
Cooling	Water
Bore and stroke	86mm bore, 92mm stroke (optionally 83mm bore, 92mm stroke)
Capacity	2138cc (optionally 1991cc)
Valves	2 valves per cylinder ohv
Compression ratio	9:1
Carburettor	2 Zenith-Stromberg 175CD
Max. power	104bhp @ 4,600rpm (optionally 100bhp @ 4,800rpm)
Max. torque	132lb ft @ 3,350rpm (optionally 117lb ft @ 3,000rpm)
Fuel capacity	11.7 gallons (53.1 litres)

Transmission

Clutch	Single dry plate, hydraulic actuation
Gearbox	S-T 4-speed with synchromesh on all forward speeds
Ratios	
1st	3.14:1
2nd	2.00:1
3rd	1.33:1
4th	1.00:1
Overdrive (optional)	0.82:1
Reverse	3.22:1
Final drive	3.7:1, 4.1:1 when overdrive fitted

Suspension and Steering

Front	Independent using unequal-length wishbones, coil springs and telescopic dampers
Rear	Independent using semi-trailing arms, coil springs and lever-arm dampers. For US market only, live axle, half-elliptic leaf springs and lever-arm dampers
Steering	Rack and pinion
Tyres	6.95–15 inch crossply
Wheels	Pressed-steel disc wheels with 4-stud fixing. Optional centre-lock wire wheels
Rim width	4 inches

Brakes

Type	Front discs, rear drums
Size	Front: 10.9 inches diameter Rear: 9.0 x 1.75 inches

Dimensions

Track	
Front	49 inches (1,245mm)
Rear	48 inches (1,220mm)
Wheelbase	88 inches (2,235mm)
Overall length	154 inches (3,910mm)
Overall width	58 inches (1,470mm)
Overall height	50 inches (1,270mm)
Unladen weight	2,240lb (1,015kg)

Performance

Top speed	109mph (175km/h)
0–60mph	10.9 sec

Inside the cockpit, the dashboard was now finished in wood and a modern 'pram'-style hood was specified in place of the earlier loose cover. The popular Surrey top was continued as an option. The handbrake, still of the 'fly-off' type, was relocated to the top of the transmission tunnel, providing for a little more leg room. Engine changes were minimal, with just a new exhaust manifold, giving a small increase in power.

TR4A – WHAT DID THEY THINK?

In September 1965, *Motor* tested a new TR4A fitted with the optional Dunlop radial tyres. A significant improvement in road-holding was reported, with suspension qualities similar to that of the 2000 saloon giving much higher levels of adhesion: 'Even on poor and mediocre surfaces found on rural country backroads the wheels stay firmly on the ground and you no longer have to eye the road ahead with suspicion.' The brakes were noted as being 'excellent', with the handling being 'enjoyable, if not the best you can buy'. An earlier review dating from March 1965 thought that the increase in power from 100bhp to 104bhp would make 'probably little difference'.

Autocar were similarly impressed with the modifications. Stuart Bladon, who had reviewed the earlier car, subsequently undertook a long journey behind the Iron Curtain in a Triumph 2000 and was quite familiar with the performance of the suspension system as fitted to that car. The magazine also noted the benefits of the softer suspension in the TR

implementation and its ability to deal with poor-quality road surfaces: 'Now the TR can be driven deliberately fast at obstacles it would have shied from before.' On the other hand, and perhaps in the interest of balance, the report commented on an increase in body roll, but also felt that 'at maximum speed in a straight line, the car [was] much more stable than a TR4'. The list price for the car tested was quoted as £800, plus purchase tax.

In the United States, the influential magazine *Road & Track* was equally impressed with the modifications, noting that the car was no longer 'hopping towards embarrassment' and concluding that 'the new suspension [was] little short of remarkable'.

At first glance, there was little to distinguish the TR4A from the TR5. The car retained the same shape and features, with some noticeable detail changes, but under the bonnet things were very different.

MORE POWER – TR5

In the mid-1960s, the wet-liner engine used in all TRs since introduction was considered to have reached the end of its life. Despite being rugged and generally reliable, it was seen as unrefined and offering no scope for further development in the chase for more power. By the time the TR4A was introduced, and since the stalwart large Standard saloon car had been superseded by the Triumph 2000 (with its more refined 6-cylinder power plant), the engine was almost unique to the

TR. Variations of it would find a home in the GT6 and Vitesse. There were also a few sales to Morgan, for fitting in their Plus 4 model. Development work at the factory had demonstrated that the bonnet of the TR could accommodate the longer 6-cylinder engine, but the 1998cc version of this engine then in production developed less power than the existing 4-cylinder engine fitted to the TR4A.

By lengthening the stroke of the engine, a useful increase in capacity to 2498cc could be achieved. In order to increase power further, fuel was to be delivered to the cylinders using a new system, developed by Lucas and named 'petrol injection'. In the mid-1960s, any reference to fuel injection meant either the sort used in diesel engines or in very specialized petrol-engined motor cars for Grand Prix racing, or those constructed by exotic continental builders. The application of petrol injection in a mass-market car was revolutionary and, as it turned out, not without its problems. In an early promotional film introducing the car that was to replace the TR4A, Raymond Baxter, in his capacity as Standard-Triumph's PR man, spoke about the new petrol-injection system as accurately measuring fuel delivery to give maximum performance while minimizing fuel consumption. The experience of some owners was quite the reverse. Nevertheless, when the system was

1 FILTER
2 MOTOR DRIVEN PUMP
3 PRESSURE RELIEF VALVE
4 SURPLUS FUEL
5 DRIVE TO ROTOR
6 METERING DISTRIBUTOR CONTROL UNIT
7 CONNECTION TO MANIFOLD
8 TO INJECTORS

TO CYLINDERS

FROM FUEL TANK

ABOVE: **The Lucas Mark 2 petrol-injection system was shown in detail inside the sales brochure for the TR5.**
© BMIHT

RIGHT: **The TR250 for the US market could be identified by the 'go-faster' stripes that, unusually, were applied transversely across the bonnet rather than along the length of the car. This example retains its original wheel covers.**

set up correctly and operating as designed, the performance increase could be quite spectacular, providing for a very fast car.

Harry Webster's engineers were fully aware of increasing constraints on exhaust emissions planned for the USA and were concerned that one downside of the Lucas petrol-injection system would be difficulties in controlling emissions to meet the new standards. For the US market, the decision was taken to fit twin Zenith-Stromberg carburettors. This unfortunately meant that the performance of the new car was no better than that of the TR4A it was to replace. It did, though, have the cachet of a 6-cylinder engine. Deviating from the established model-naming strategy and to identify this new model as a US-only product, while injected cars were marketed as 'TR5 PI', US-market cars were given the name 'TR 250'.

ABOVE LEFT: **TR 250s were fitted with this bonnet badge...**

ABOVE RIGHT: **... whereas the TR5 was badged with a similar TR5 badge. In both cases the badge was located off-centre.**

ABOVE LEFT: **From the rear, the TR5 boasted of its PI (petrol-injection) system...**

ABOVE RIGHT: **... while the TR 250 just announced its model description. Overdrive was an option on both cars. Reversing lights are now fitted.**

Triumph TR5 – Original Specification

Layout and Chassis
Two-seat sports car with separate chassis

Engine

Type	Standard-Triumph 6 cylinder in-line
Block material	Cast iron
Head material	Cast iron
Cylinders	6 in-line
Cooling	Water
Bore and stroke	74.7mm bore, 95mm stroke
Capacity	2498cc
Valves	2 valves per cylinder ohv
Compression ratio	9.5:1
Fuel supply	Lucas Mark 2 fuel injection
Max. power	150bhp @ 5,000rpm
Max. torque	164lb ft @ 3,500rpm
Fuel capacity	11.2 gallons (51 litres)

Transmission

Clutch	Single dry plate, hydraulic actuation
Gearbox	S-T 4-speed with synchromesh on all forward speeds
Ratios	
1st	3.14:1
2nd	2.00:1
3rd	1.33:1
4th	1.00:1
Overdrive (optional)	0.82:1
Reverse	3.22:1
Final drive	3.45:1

Suspension and Steering

Front	Independent using unequal-length wishbones, coil springs and telescopic dampers
Rear	Independent using semi-trailing arms, coil springs and lever-arm dampers
Steering	Rack and pinion
Tyres	165R–15in radial
Wheels	Pressed-steel disc wheels with 4-stud fixing. Optional centre-lock wire wheels
Rim width	4.5 inches

Brakes

Type	Front discs, rear drums
Size	
Front:	10.9 inches diameter
Rear:	9.0 x 1.75 inches

Dimensions

Track	
Front	49.25 inches (1,250mm)
Rear	48.75 inches (1,240mm)
Wheelbase	88 inches (2,235mm)
Overall length	154 inches (3,910mm)
Overall width	58 inches (1,470mm)
Overall height	50 inches (1,270mm)
Unladen weight	2,268lb (1,043kg)

Performance

Top speed	125mph (200km/h) (Triumph figures)
0–60mph	8.8 sec

Triumph TR 250 – Original Specification

Specification as TR5 except where noted:

Engine

Compression ratio 8.5:1	
Carburettors	2 Zenith-Stromberg 175CD2SE
Max. power	104bhp @ 4,500rpm
Max. torque	143lb ft @ 3,000rpm

Transmission

Final drive	3.7:1

Suspension and Steering

Tyres	185R–15in radial

Performance

Top speed	107mph (172km/h)
0–60mph	10.6 sec

CAVEAT EMPTOR! (LET THE BUYER BEWARE)

Of all Triumph cars, and TRs in particular, the increase in value of TR5s has been the most spectacular. Perhaps because of their rarity, having been in production for such a short period of time, or perhaps because of the combination of performance coupled with the elegant Michelotti body style, the TR5 has become a highly desirable car to both enthusiasts and collectors. With so few genuine TR5s built and a much larger number of TR 250s reimported from the USA, the temptation is there to recreate a TR5 by installing a TR6 engine and associated equipment. Doing the homework on any classic-car purchase is important and, in the case of a TR5, absolutely essential.

Originally a US-specification TR 250 car, this example has been restored as a right-hand-drive car and retains all its original badges, allowing for a correct identification. Although never sold outside of the USA, TR 250s are sought-after classic cars, combining the Michelotti body style and smooth 6-cylinder engine. TONY ALDERTON

Other than the engine changes, significant modifications were limited to the substitution of the dynamo by an alternator and the standard fit of a vacuum servo to boost braking. With the amount of power available, this was perhaps considered to be an essential item that should not be offered as an option. A new design of steering wheel was also provided and minor changes were made to the detail external fittings to the car. The front grille had the top surface of its slats finished in satin black. The bonnet badge was moved to one side, trapezoidal in shape and bearing the legend 'TR5' or 'TR 250', while badges with the logo '2500' were fitted to the trailing ends of the rear wings along with side marker lamps. Most noticeably, TR 250 models were decorated with a 'racing' stripe on the bonnet. Unusually, instead of running the length of the car, this ran transversely across the bonnet and down the wings.

For once, there was no demand from the US dealer network for a reduced-cost option and all TR5/TR 250 models were fitted with independent coil spring rear suspension in the style developed for the TR4A.

TR5 AND TR 250 – ON TEST

It was 'the answer to the enthusiast's prayer', according to *Motor*, which mentioned the effortless torque and the melodious exhaust that 'must delight even the most decibel-conscious ear'. There were a few negative points: the lumpy idle as a result of the 'hairy' camshaft timing and the tendency of the tail to dip when accelerating hard. There was also some scuttle shake.

Autocar thought the car was 'a complete transformation', making note of the smooth and vivid acceleration, the light gear change, good road-holding and gearing that provided for a cruising speed of 100mph. The engine came in for special mention: 'the heart of a car is its engine and the TR5 has an eager unit which responds just as a sports car driver wants'. The magazine *Autosport* also reported a test on the car, which was equally positive and ended with a prophetic comment: 'Fuel injection adds interest to the specification but above all it improves the performance and the flexibility. Very soon, a prestige car without fuel injection will be unthinkable.'

At the time of the first tests, in April 1968, the home-market list price of the TR5 was £985, plus purchase tax of £275 13s 1d.

Reviews in the United States were not quite so positive. The appearance of the car was much the same, the performance more or less identical and perhaps there had been the expectation of something better. *Road & Track* in a December 1967 feature were as usual complimentary to the Triumph product and concluded a generally upbeat review with the words 'everything that was done by the TR4A is done more easily and smoothly by the TR250'. However, the reporter did express some disappointment that an entirely new model was not forthcoming, and felt that the 'body structure [was] well behind modern standards'. The following April, *Motor Trend* mentioned the omission of petrol injection for US models as 'a fact that is still difficult to comprehend'.

Later in 1968, *Motor* took six contemporary sports cars – the TR5, Lotus Elan S4, Marcos 1600, Jaguar E-Type, Mercedes-Benz 280SL and AC Fastback – on a group test. The results showed very clearly what remarkably good value for money the TR5 represented. Against an 'on the road as tested' price of £1,261 for the TR, the Lotus would relieve a potential owner of £1,732 and the Jaguar £2,225. *Three* TR5s could be had for the cost of the 280SL, with its list price of £4,154.

The side view of the car changed very little from that of the TR4A. '2500' badges and rear side marker lights were added and the door lock was moved from the door handle.

Another new radiator grille. This time, there was no provision for a starting handle, although the lower pressing from the earlier car was retained, as was the indent for the handle.

There was little change to the dashboard or instruments, with no more than a tidying-up of the switchgear. The face-level ventilators became 'eyeball' ones and the instruments were given a black surround. This car also has an after-market steering wheel fitted – the 1960s driving gloves are an essential accessory.

PETROL INJECTION – THE ACHILLES HEEL

Today, with the modifications made to the Triumph PI cars, the difficulties experienced with the original system are beginning to fade. While the typical dealer mechanic of the era was suf-

ficiently skilled to deal with the adjustments needed to keep cars fitted with twin carburettors in perfect tune, the techniques that were required to be applied to the Lucas system were more akin to aviation than motor cars. Coupled with numerous compromises in the design to reduce the cost and a lack of training of the dealer staff, the PI cars, both TR5 and the recently introduced 2.5PI saloons, using fundamentally the same 2498cc engine and injection equipment, soon developed an unwelcome reputation for poor reliability and heavy fuel consumption. Some dealers even developed a conversion kit to replace the injection system with twin carburettors, trading performance for reliability.

The origins of the Lucas system had been established in the military market, where cost was less of an issue, and had been adapted to power certain race cars built by Jaguar and Maserati. The application by Triumph was a first for any type of fuel injection on a mass-market car and the level of detail and precision required were perhaps not fully understood.

The engine compartment of the TR5 became a little more complicated with the addition of the petrol-injection system. In this example, the orange 'leads' crossing the top of the engine are high-pressure hoses delivering fuel to the injectors; an additional vacuum hose provides information on engine load and fuel requirements to the metering unit. The large black tube is a plenum chamber supplying air to each of the six throttle butterflies.

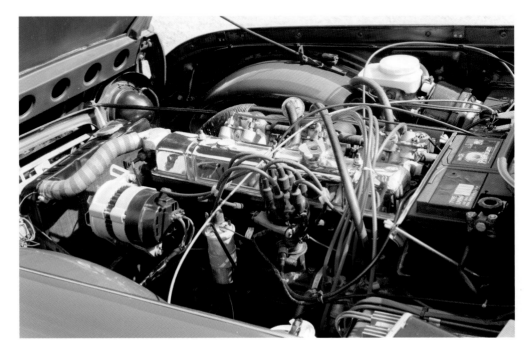

Viewed from the other side of the engine, the metering unit can be seen below and just behind the distributor; both were operated and timed from the camshaft. A Lucas alternator now became a standard fitting, replacing the outdated dynamo of earlier cars.

The system required a high-pressure fuel pump. To meet cost imperatives, this was based on that most familiar of Lucas components, the windscreen-wiper motor. Located above the exhaust silencer in the boot, the fuel pump suffered both from a lack of precision in assembly and overheating in operation. The system also pumped excess fuel back into the tank. This fuel, having been pumped at high pressure, was warmed and splashed back into the tank, creating aeration and frothing. While the tank was full, this was not a serious problem as the volume of fuel would absorb the excess air and heat; however, as the tank emptied, the fuel would increase in temperature and become more aerated. It soon became common practice not to allow the fuel tank to become less than one-quarter full. The design of the tank, lacking baffles and a small sump, accentuated the problem when fuel levels were low, as a sweeping left-hand bend would cause the remaining tank content to move to the right and partial fuel starvation to occur. The fuel pump had a tendency to overheat and apocryphal stories abound of Triumph owners resorting to packets of frozen peas in order to cool an overheated pump. A cooling coil was quickly adapted to provide additional cooling, but using the returning fuel to act as the coolant transferred the excess heat from the pump motor to the fuel, further increasing its temperature and tendency to vaporize.

At the engine end, each cylinder was provided with an individual injector and air supply was provided by six butterfly throttles, arranged as three groups, with each group individually adjustable. Perfect synchronization of the throttles was essential for smooth performance. The delivery of fuel to the injectors was controlled within the metering unit by a rotating shuttle, driven via a gearing from the ignition distributor, and the actual amount of fuel delivered was dictated by the current engine vacuum, controlled though a mechanical linkage. Tolerances within the metering unit had to be controlled precisely to within thousandths of an inch and were not ideally adjusted within the typical 1960s dealer workshop. Today, prior to any adjustments being made to the injection system it is absolutely essential for the engine to be in good order overall – correct valve clearances, exact ignition timing and fully working electrical system. Once these points are put right, the majority of injection problems resolve themselves, provided the temptation to adjust the petrol system can be resisted.

Even as the TR5/TR 250 was being developed, Triumph were anxiously looking at what was to replace the design,

One of the three throttle bodies, each containing a pair of butterflies and two injectors. Balancing the airflow to each throttle body was essential if the engine was to run smoothly. Setting the idle speed on a TR5 required the butterflies to be adjusted to allow just sufficient airflow for the engine to idle smoothly. A cigarette paper is often advised as a suitable feeler gauge.

The engine compartment of a TR 250 is a much simpler affair, with twin carburettors replacing the PI system.
TONY ALDERTON

which was now nearing its seventh birthday. At the dawn of the 1960s, a new body style had replaced the side-screen cars, but the mechanical parts had remained almost unchanged. Independent rear suspension had given a welcome improvement to handling and with the TR5 Triumph had introduced a dramatic increase in power. By 1967, the Michelotti body design, although much admired then as now, was a familiar sight and consequently the next change was going to be to the body as the Triumph TR evolved to move into the 1970s.

CHAPTER SIX

TRIUMPH IN THE ALPS – TR4s IN COMPETITION

The Michelotti-designed cars rack up sporting achievements in European rallying and circuit racing, then and now.

With the closure of the Competitions Department, following the success at Le Mans in 1961, it looked as though works-sponsored competition for Triumph had come to an end. For a company producing motor cars with such a strong sporting character and successful heritage in motorsport it was almost inconceivable that such a situation could exist for long. Sure enough, in 1962, Technical Director for Standard-Triumph

Harry Webster set up a new Competitions Department, appointing recently recruited development engineer Graham Robson as Competitions Secretary. With minimal funding and few resources, the new Triumph works team would run a fleet of the new TR4 cars, registered 3VC, 4VC, 5VC and 6VC. Their livery was to be powder blue, a colour that would reproduce well in the monochrome newspapers and journals of the day.

LEFT: **6VC is one of the original TR4 rally cars and still competes in historic rally events.**

OPPOSITE PAGE TOP: **The dashboard and interior of 6VC retain many of the original features, although the roll cage is a modern fitting for compliance with current standards for participation in motorsport.**

BELOW LEFT: The cars were fitted with long-range fuel tanks. The majority of the fuel volume was now cantilevered out from the mounting points, requiring a support bar to be fitted underneath to prevent the mounts from fracturing.

BOTTOM LEFT: An 'ammo box' and clips were fitted in the boot to carry spares and tools on events.

BELOW RIGHT: The gear lever was modified into this cranked arrangement.

SUCCESS ON A SHOESTRING

With the closure of the earlier Competitions Department, all the records had been lost or destroyed, but it was a known fact within Triumph that the TR2 and TR3 rally cars had been essentially standard production models with minimal adaptation to prepare them for the rigours of rallying. This extended to performance tuning the 4-cylinder wet-liner engine; despite the large number of privately entered cars racing in a higher state of tune, the expertise was outside rather than within the company. One such source of expertise was within the firm of SAH Accessories, owned by Syd Hurrell, who produced various components including suitable inlet manifolds to allow the use of high-performance Weber carburettors and more aggressively profiled camshafts. An agreement was reached whereby Hurrell's business would provide the works team with these and other components in return for publicity. The Competitions Department would deal with the issue of homologation.

Elsewhere in the organization, lightweight alloy body panels were obtained and perspex replaced glass in the windows. Other vehicles provided differential gears so that various back-axle ratios could be homologated and Laycock built heavy-duty overdrives that could be used with all forward speeds, effectively providing eight gear ratios. Superfluous trim removal balanced the additional weight of body strengthening and underbody shields, to ensure that the weight of the rally car was similar to that of the road-going version.

Crews were paid an allowance for their expenses, but were not on contract and were not paid any fees. It was all in dramatic contrast with the massive budgets involved in works-sponsored motorsport today; nevertheless, the results obtained by Triumph's Competition Department with the fleet of TR4s were impressive.

The Tulip Rally of 1962 was to be the first outing for the powder blue TR4s, with 3VC driven by John Sprinzel, 4VC driven by Mike Sutcliffe and Jean-Jacques Thuner in charge of 5VC. All three cars were fitted with the lightened body panels and at this stage of their careers were running standard 2-litre engines. The team achieved second, third and fourth in class.

TRIUMPH AGAIN IN THE ALPS

Next it was off to the French Alps for the 1962 Alpine Rally. By now, all the works cars had been equipped with the 2.2-litre engines. The crews were Sprinzel and Cave in 3VC, Sutcliffe and Fidler in 4VC and Thuner and Gretener in 5VC. The fourth car, 6VC, was nominally held as a spare and used for reconnaissance purposes in connection with the 1962 Alpine. For publicity reasons, Triumph's PR department requested that 6VC be made available to a team comprising of Tommy Wisdom and Jeff Uren. Wisdom began his rallying career in the 1930s and, having achieved success in previous winter rallies, was motoring correspondent of *The Daily Herald*. Uren was a saloon-car racer and had been Competitions Manager for Ford. Despite being something of a publicity entry, the car finished close behind the others. Sprinzel's car did not finish the event, having been involved in an accident in the Dolomites. In an event noted for its difficulty and in a year in which fewer than half the entrants finished, it was remarkable that the TR4s should achieve first, second and third in class and that Mike Sutcliffe should be awarded a 'Coupe des Alpes' (Alpine Cup) for his penalty-free completion of the event.

NEW DRIVERS

In 1963, two new drivers, Roger Clark and Brian Culcheth, were engaged for the Liège–Sofia–Liège rally. This was to be the only event in which either driver was to compete in a works TR4, in this case in 4VC. (Brian later achieved great success for the works team driving a Triumph 2.5PI saloon to second overall place in the 1970 London to Mexico World Cup Rally and later returned to TRs as a driver in the works TR7. Roger Clark was to achieve his most noteworthy success driving for the Ford works team, especially in the highly competitive Escort and eventually again for Triumph in TR7v8s.)

The car was withdrawn from the event in Yugoslavia having suffered a broken gearbox, and the two other TR4s entered also failed to finish. In any case it was becoming clear that the world of rallying was changing. Events were becoming much tougher on the cars, with a greater use of rough roads that did not particularly suit low sports cars, and races being run on handicap, which tended to penalize sports cars. The results list for 1963 shows a higher number of 'DNF' (Did Not Finish) than in previous years.

For the TR4s, as for the earlier TR2s and TR3s, the main competitor was the Austin-Healey 3000, which had now

An original sticker from the
1963 Liège–Sofia rally in the rear
screen of 6VC.

Roger Clark and Brian Culcheth
at the start of the 1963 Liège–
Sofia event; the only time that
either were to compete in a
TR4.
BRIAN CULCHETH

grown in power to something in excess of 200bhp. The TR4s were faster and more rugged than the side-screen cars of the previous era, but the competition had moved on as well, with serious competition from Alfa-Romeo and Porsche to contend with. It became increasingly apparent to the management of the company that the TR had no serious future in rallying, which was quickly changing to a sport no longer for series production cars but for specialist cars, dominated by the likes of the Mini-Cooper and Lotus-Cortina. The swan-song of the powder blue TR4s was to be in North America for the 1964 five-day Shell 4000 Rally, at the time the longest event in the world, at over 4,000 miles (6,400km).

BRIAN CULCHETH JOINS TRIUMPH

Brian Culcheth was employed selling cars in 1963 and had already had some success in motorsport when he was approached by Graham Robson as Triumph's Competition Secretary to participate in the 1963 Liège with Roger Clark, another young rally driver who was to achieve great fame and success in the coming years. Brian recalls the event as being particularly arduous, held over five days with just one hour's official rest time.

At the time of his appointment to the team, Brian recalls that Vic Elford and Terry Hunter had been dispatched to perform a reconnaissance of the route. 'I'm not really sure what they were recce'ing,' says Brian, 'I think it might have

STANDARD-TRIUMPH ENGINEERING LIMITED

TELEPHONE : COVENTRY 75533
TELEGRAMS : STACK COVENTRY

FLETCHAMSTEAD
COVENTRY
ENGLAND

B.Culcheth Esq,
c/o John Sprinzel (Racing) Ltd.,
32 Lancaster Mews,
LONDON W2.

12th July 1963.

Dear Brian,

I am writing to confirm the remarks made on the telephone yesterday, namely that we would like to invite you to co-drive with Roger Clark in a TR4 on the Liege-Sofia-Liege Rally at the end of August.

We will pay all your expenses,at the rate of £7 per day whilst away with the cars,and all travel and hotel bookings will be made in advance.

When I receive the entry form duly completed by Roger Clark I will forward it to you,and would be obliged if you could fill in the appropriate details,such as address,competition number etc.Please remember also to include a passport photograph when you return the completed Entry Form as this will be required for the Rally road book.

Roger Clark is going off on a recce trip with Vic and Terry Hunter, on the 31st July for 10days.

If there are any queries please get in touch with me as soon as possible,

Yours sincerely,
for STANDARD TRIUMPH ENGINEERING LTD.,

A.A.G.Robson.
Competition Secretary.

A MEMBER OF THE STANDARD-TRIUMPH GROUP

A very rare artefact from 1963: Brian Culcheth's letter of engagement for the event that he drove with Roger Clark.
BRIAN CULCHETH

Reunited with 4VC, Brian Culcheth stands next to the driver's door, along with Ian Cornish, the long-time owner of the car.

been bars and nightclubs, because the information we got on the actual route and conditions was a bit vague, but they did seem to have a good knowledge of the entertainment on offer all along the route.' 'This was the first time that the TRs

had been entered with the 2.2-litre engine, but we broke he gearbox and that was the end of the event for us'. 'Graham [Robson] didn't keep either of us on the team afterwards.'

The strongest competition to the TRs came from the Austin-Healey 3000. This is perhaps one of the most famous of them all, driven to great success by Pat Moss and Ann Wisdom, both of whom had experience earlier with TRs.

TR4s IN CANADA

The three cars, 3, 5 and 6VC, were rebuilt over the winter of 1963–64 into left-hand-drive configuration and shipped initially to California where they were delivered to the workshops of 'Kas' Kastner. Kastner at the time was Standard-Triumph's North American Competitions Manager and had a reputation for being able to tune engines to wrestle the very last measure of power from them. Re-registered in the State of Oregon as CAG 408, CAG 409 and CAG 410, the cars were then transported to Vancouver, British Columbia, the starting point of the Shell 4000 Rally.

3VC was driven by Bert Rasmussen, an employee of Standard-Triumph (Canada) who had achieved success in local rally events. It completed the event, finishing 16th overall. 5VC finished in 21st position, driven by long-time Triumph driver Jean-Jacques Thuner, and 6VC was driven to 17th position by Gordon Jennings, editor of the US magazine

Car & Driver – with a view to receiving positive reports, no doubt.

The three cars and crews achieved the GT team prize, demonstrating that, while Triumph and the TRs could not always be expected to achieve outright wins, the record of success in team competitions continued to the end of separate chassis TR rallying. This was to be the final factory-sponsored event for the team cars, which were eventually sold into private ownership. Three of the four cars have returned to the UK and are now in private ownership. 5VC was believed to have been dismantled in North America, although a car claiming to be that vehicle has emerged in Germany.

TR4s ON THE CIRCUIT IN NORTH AMERICA

Other than the expeditions to Le Mans, the focus of the Triumph works team was on the rally circuit, but in North

KASTNER – THE TUNING LEGEND

R.W. 'Kas' Kastner's first competition success came in 1952 when he won a street race in Aspen, Colorado, driving his MG TD. He immediately developed a reputation as someone who 'knew about engines' and who could tune them to achieve maximum power. With a family to support, he set up his own tuning business in Salt Lake City, but immediately ran into a problem in that the cars that he had repaired and improved tended to stay repaired and improved. When an opportunity to work for a British car dealership arose, Kastner and family relocated to Los Angeles, which led to an offer to work as Service Manager for CAL Sales, the Triumph agent and distributor for the western United States. Kastner's racing continued, now in a TR3, but when CAL Sales was acquired by Triumph and a rule was imposed that managers could not enter competitive motorsport, that part of his career came to an end.

In the true Californian spirit of the entrepreneur, Kastner manufactured performance components in his garage, even selling them to his employer. His garage also tuned and improved the engines that were to power the cars to team success in the 12 Hours at Sebring in 1963. A showdown

ensued with Triumph America when Kastner asked for some recompense for his own time spent in preparing the cars and was told that there would be nothing forthcoming. Not unreasonably, Kastner considered his options and decided to take up an offer from Carroll Shelby to run his team at a vastly increased salary. Triumph reconsidered their position and, prior to Kastner commencing with Shelby, an accommodation was reached, resulting in Kastner heading Triumph's North American Competitions Department, a first for any foreign car manufacturer in the United States.

'Kas' also became an accomplished writer, both of magazine articles and of the definitive books on tuning Triumph engines for performance. He remained with Triumph until 1970 when he was offered a position overseeing all motorsport activities for what had by then become British Leyland. Foreseeing what would eventually befall the Coventry company, Kastner left Triumph to set up his own racing team and to develop aftermarket turbo-charging systems for performance cars. Before finally retiring, he led Nissan to competition success in the United States.

America success was to be had with the TR in circuit racing under the leadership of R.W. 'Kas' Kastner. In 1963, a team of three TR4s was prepared and entered into the twelve-hour race held at Sebring, Florida. A former airfield converted into a racetrack, utilizing runways and perimeter roads as part of the circuit and noted for its rough surface, Sebring provides a testing environment for any car, especially in conjunction with the Florida climate. Completion of the twelve-hour event is testimony to the ruggedness and reliability of a car. It was therefore a notable achievement in 1963, when the TR4s finished in first, second and fourth places in their class, although the overall winner was a Ferrari 250P driven by John Surtees.

A TR4 at the Silverstone circuit during the annual Silverstone Classic shows. TR4s remain a popular choice for competitors in modern-day classic sports-car racing.

CHAPTER SEVEN

KAMM TAILS AND KARMANN – THE TR6

A new, more brutal appearance is launched for the TR range. Retaining many of the features of the TR5, the front and rear of the car are revised to give a new shape more in keeping with the 1970s. The TR6 goes on to outsell all earlier separate chassis TRs and earn itself the title of the 'last of the hairy-chested sports cars'.

The next evolution of the TR needs to be placed within the context of the changes that were happening in the British motor industry in the late 1960s. Strikes and troubled labour relations had been part of the industrial scene throughout the 1960s and it could be considered that the entire British motor industry had become complacent about its market share and continuing existence. The acquisition of Standard-Triumph by Leyland Motors was just one example of the mergers and acquisitions that had been happening among Midlands-based manufacturing companies. In 1952, Austin and the Nuffield Group (Morris, Wolseley, Riley and MG predominantly) merged to form the British Motor Corporation. Leonard Lord, of Austin, had previously been an employee of William Morris and the merger brought together two businesses that encompassed many rivalries, both commercial and personal. Those rivalries were to have an impact on Triumph far into the future.

Jaguar purchased Daimler from BSA and made a move in the commercial vehicle market by acquiring the insolvent Guy Motors business. It also made investments in more specialist areas, with the takeover of Coventry Climax and Henry Meadows Ltd, both established engine manufacturers of great repute. The US-owned businesses of Ford and General Motors, in the guise of Vauxhall in Britain, were significant players in the market for both cars and light commercials. The Rootes Group were coming more under the control of the Chrysler Corporation of the United States, which had been increasing its ownership throughout the 1960s.

Of all these groupings, BMC retained the position of being the largest producer of vehicles and, while there were to be no more significant mergers under the BMC name, the acquisition of Pressed Steel created a problem for other manufacturers, which were rightly concerned that future designs could become known to their competitors. In 1966, Jaguar and BMC merged to form British Motor Holdings, leaving just Rover as an independent volume producer of motor cars. Rover was rapidly folded into the Leyland Motors empire and, with persuasion from the government under the influence of Prime Minister Harold Wilson, Leyland Motors and BMH merged to form British Leyland.

It was in the context of this turmoil that the new and future TRs were to be designed. Due to increasing work commitments, Triumph were unable to secure the services of Giovanni Michelotti, but found that Wilhelm Karmann GmbH, based in Osnabruck in what was then called West Germany, could undertake a restyle and manufacture new press tools. Approval for the design was given in September 1967 and it was planned to introduce the new car in January 1969. With its squared-off design and distinctive Kamm tail, the car looked entirely new.

THE NEW TR EMERGES

Close examination reveals that the centre section of the earlier Michelotti-designed cars had been retained; it was only the extremities that had been revised but the overall effect

ABOVE: **'The last of the hairy-chested sports cars': a 1974 model TR6, previously owned by the author.**

RIGHT: **While the centre cockpit section of the car was carried over relatively unchanged other than the deletion of the bright work, the new front and rear gave the TR6 a completely different profile. The alloy wheels are a later addition.**

met the market expectations of an entirely new car. Mechanical changes were minor, with the Lucas petrol-injection system retained for markets except the United States, where a carburetted engine was continued. Badging was amended so that the 'PI' tag was lost and the script 'injection' was added under the rear manufacturer's badge. A front anti-roll bar was added as standard. Early cars featured a body-coloured windscreen frame in the same manner as the outgoing

Triumph TR6 PI – Original Specification

Layout and Chassis
Two-seat sports car with separate chassis

Engine
Type	Standard-Triumph 6-cylinder in-line
Block material	Cast iron
Head material	Cast iron
Cylinders	6 in-line
Cooling	Water
Bore and stroke	74.7mm bore, 95mm stroke
Capacity	2498cc
Valves	2 valves per cylinder ohv
Compression ratio	9.5:1
Fuel supply	Lucas Mark 2 fuel injection
Max. power	150bhp @ 5,000rpm CP series
	124bhp DIN @ 5,000rpm CR series
Max. torque	164lb ft @ 3,500rpm CP series
	143lb ft @ 3,500rpm CR series
Fuel capacity	11.2 gallons (51 litres)

Transmission
Clutch	Single dry plate, hydraulic actuation
Gearbox	S-T 4-speed with synchromesh on all forward speeds

Ratios (up to mid-1971)
1st	3.14:1
2nd	2.00:1
3rd	1.33:1
4th	1.00:1
Overdrive (optional)	0.82:1
Reverse	3.22:1
Final drive	3.45:1

Ratios (mid-1971 onwards)
1st	2.99:1
2nd	2.10:1
3rd	1.39:1
4th	1.00:1

Overdrive (optional)	0.82:1 (0.797 from commission number CR567)
Reverse	3.77:1

Suspension and Steering
Front	Independent using unequal-length wishbones, coil springs and telescopic dampers. Anti-roll bar
Rear	Independent using semi-trailing arms, coil springs and lever-arm dampers
Steering	Rack and pinion
Tyres	165R–15in radial
Wheels	Pressed-steel disc wheels with 4-stud fixing. Optional centre-lock wire wheels
Rim width	5.5 inches

Brakes
Type	Front discs, rear drums
Size	Front: 10.9 inches diameter
	Rear: 9.0 x 1.75 inches

Dimensions
Track
Front	50.25 inches (1,275mm)
Rear	48.75 inches (1,240mm)
Wheelbase	88 inches (2,235mm)
Overall length	159 inches (4,040mm)
Overall width	58 inches (1,470mm)
Overall height	50 inches (1,270mm)
Unladen weight	2,408lb (1,085kg)

Performance
Top speed	119mph (191km/h) (CP series)
	116mph (186km/h) (CR series)
0–60mph	8.2 sec (CP series)
	9.5 sec (CR series)

models, but this was soon modified to a semi-matt black finish, complementing the finish applied to the Kamm tail. The model names were also tidied, with both injected and carburetted cars known officially as 'TR6', although, inevitably, the market has come to differentiate the models as 'TR6' and 'TR6 PI'. One significant difference between the new car and its predecessor was the deletion of the Surrey top option, which was replaced with a traditional steel hard top.

RIGHT: **The Surrey roof was unique to the Michelotti designs; the TR6 reverted to the traditional hard top.**

BELOW LEFT: **Rear view of a TR6 showing the new lighting arrangements, which were larger than those used on earlier cars. They were also wrapped around, in order to meet the legal requirements in some countries for turn signals to be visible from the side as well as the rear. On cars destined for the USA, the amber repeater was replaced with a side marker lamp.**

ABOVE RIGHT: **Earlier cars had the number-plate lamp fitted to the rear bumper and illuminating upwards; later cars had the lamps set into the overlap of the boot lid. The rear panel on all TR6s was painted in satin black although some owners in modern times have chosen to paint this panel in body colour.**

The TR6, the final separate-chassis TR, was destined to sell in the highest numbers of any TR to date and to be built for the longest period. Unsurprisingly, the car was subject to a continuous programme of change and improvement during its lifetime. Some of this was in order to refresh its appeal in the market and some to keep in line with legislative and environmental restrictions, particularly in the USA. A significant change occurred around November 1972 when a revised car was first delivered. Identified formally by a change in commission number prefix from CP to CR for injected cars, and CC to CF for US-market cars, it had a small front spoiler added under the front bumper. The rear number-plate light, previously positioned in the rear bumper, had been moved into the boot lid and minor changes had also occurred in the cabin with new switches.

Significantly, a modified engine was also fitted to injected cars, with a softer cam timing to increase the drivability of the car, especially in traffic. On paper, this reduced the maximum power of the injected engine from 150bhp to 125bhp. Over the years, various myths have surrounded this change – perhaps it pointed to a need to ensure that the ageing TR model range did not offer more horsepower than the flagship Stag with its 3-litre V8 engine. Whatever the reasons for it, the decrease in power was not quite as significant

as it appeared because the early measurement was to SAE standard whereas the later number was measured using the more conservative DIN standard. However, the change to performance data clearly shows that the newer cars were, at the limit, not as fast as the early TR6 or TR5. Somewhat disingenuously, the later sales brochures for the TR6 make no reference to engine power – a remarkable omission considering the intended market for the car.

A new model of overdrive was fitted, still supplied by Laycock de Normanville, with the long-serving 'A' type replaced by the newer 'J' type and operation restricted to third and top gear. An earlier change had rationalized gear-change ratios, providing commonality with other cars being built by Triumph at the time, if not total interchangeability of gearbox assemblies.

During this period, design work was being carried out for the successor car, which would be a monocoque of completely new design, and expenditure on significant changes to the TR6 was denied, with only modifications to detail and to accommodate new legislation being approved. Of course, the turmoil of the new British Leyland organization was also going on in the background. Later US models received bracing in the doors to minimize intrusion in the event of a side impact, and the door design was changed for all markets to include a small pull handle. Earlier cars had relied on an

ABOVE LEFT: **Black-rimmed dials were used on the early cars and the needles on the minor gauges pointed downwards. Lighting was controlled by the left stalk while the wipers and screen washers used separate switches located at the extreme right edge of the attractive wooden dashboard.**

ABOVE RIGHT: **Later cars used chromed rims to the instruments. The needles pointed upwards and a voltmeter replaced the ammeter. Lights were now controlled by a rocker switch and a combined wiper and washer switch was positioned below this. The ignition switch was now positioned below the steering column where it also operated a steering lock.**

Revisions to the height of the front bumper necessitated a change to the front marker and turn signal lamps.

Later low-impact safety revisions for US cars required large rubber over-riders to be fitted, as seen on this very late US model TR6, parked among a selection of much earlier TRs.

inset hand grip moulded into a finisher fitted at the top of the door frame. It was only just adequate and it was not unknown for passengers to attempt to use a door pocket to close the door, with the result that the door pocket would

be torn off. The door-top mouldings were also prone to falling off or, more likely, being pulled off.

US-market cars gained additional equipment in the engine bay to reduce emissions, particularly for the key California

Triumph TR6 US Models – Original Specification

As TR6 PI except as noted:

Layout and Chassis
Two-seat sports car with separate chassis

Engine

Compression ratio	8.5:1 to 1972, 7.75:1 to 1973, 7.5:1 thereafter
Carburettors	2 Zenith-Stromberg 175CD2SE, 175CD2SEV from 1973–76
Max. power	104bhp @ 4,500rpm, increased to 106bhp @ 4,900rpm from 1972
Max. torque	143lb ft @ 3,000rpm, 133lb ft @ 3,000rpm from 1972

Transmission
Ratios

Final drive	3.45:1

Suspension and Steering

Tyres	185R–15in radial

Dimensions

Overall length	159 inches (4,040mm), increasing in stages to 163.5 inches (4,155mm) with impact protection over-riders
Unladen weight	2,268lb (1,034kg), increasing to 2,442lb (1,106kg)

Performance

Top speed	111mph (177km/h)
0–60mph	10.7 sec (CC series)
	11.5 sec (CF series)

CHANGES TO THE PETROL-INJECTION SYSTEM

The original design specification of the Lucas petrol-injection system was based around a single butterfly to control airflow, a system that is now widely used in modern implementations of fuel injection. Triumph had chosen to use a butterfly per cylinder, immediately complicating the set-up and synchronization of airflow across each cylinder. Initially, the throttles were worked

by a common linkage connected to the butterflies by rods, each adjustable for length to provide synchronization. Each pair of butterflies was fitted with an adjustment screw to provide a small air bleed for idle and, with careful adjustment to provide perfect synchronization, a smooth idle and pick-up could be achieved. Once these adjustments were set, a master adjustment under the linkage provided for in-service adjustment of idle speed, but this was difficult to access. Subsequently, an air-bleed valve was fitted to the end of the balance pipe connected between the three throttle bodies and the butterflies could then be adjusted to be just closed at normal idle speed.

At about the time of the introduction of the CR model range, the throttle bodies and linkage were modified. These later throttle bodies can be identified by their two balance pipes. In addition, the linkage was modified so that, instead of a common linkage operating all butterflies, the linkage was split into three. This was arranged so that movement of the first section would operate the second and third sections. All was fine until the system developed normal wear in service, resulting in the butterflies no longer operating in synchronization.

ABOVE LEFT: **One modification to the TR6 injection system was the addition of this bleed valve. Throttle butterflies could now be fully closed at idle speed and airflow adjusted through this valve to control idle speed.**

LEFT: **Under the bonnet, very little changed between the TR5 and TR6. Later injection systems can be identified easily by the presence of a second balance pipe between the three throttle bodies.**

A close-up view of the metering unit fitted to the Lucas petrol-injection system.

market, which was leading the way in environmental controls, and to encompass safety legislation. US cars were also fitted with different seats incorporating large fixed headrests, the height of the front bumpers was revised and, from late 1974, large black bumper over-riders were fitted to absorb the energy from low-speed impacts. Alterations to the bumper heights also had an effect on the positioning and style of the front indicator lamps.

TR6 PRESS REACTION

Ask a Triumph enthusiast to describe the TR6 and the expression 'the last of the hairy-chested sports cars' will inevitably come up. This well-worn phrase probably has its origins in a road test published in *Autocar* in April 1969. With the demise of the Austin Healey 3000, the mantle of the powerful, large-engined sports car that was, allegedly, difficult to control, passed to the TR6. The preamble to *Autocar*'s road test described the car as 'very much a masculine machine, calling for beefy muscles, bold decisions and even ruthlessness on occasions'. *Motor*'s June 1969 issue picked up the theme, with a reference to 'old he-man feel', and Austral-

ian journal *Sports Car World* described the car as being 'For Men Only' in the title of an article published six months later: 'One manufacturer is keeping the tradition of the hairy-chested sports car alive. The Triumph TR6 is a man's car all the way down the line.' The same magazine used the 'hairy-chested sports car' tag again just over a year later in a road test, and it reappeared in June 1971, when the glossy magazine *CAR* undertook a 'Giant Test' between a Lotus Elan Sprint and TR6. In *CAR*'s opinion, the test confirmed the Triumph as 'the undisputed holder of the Last of the Hairy-Chested Sports Cars title'.

With the differences between the TR5 and TR6 mainly involving the body styling, the printed reviews tended to focus on this area, although the modification to the front suspension, with the addition of an anti-roll bar, came in for comment from *Motor*. They tested the car in June 1969, noting 'better stability on fast corners, as well as [a reduction in] the tendency for the nose to tuck in sharply when the throttle [was] lifted on sharper corners'. They also mentioned the effect of the front anti-roll bar in providing more understeer and the wider tyres fitted as standard, to give more grip in all conditions. Commenting on the evolution of TRs over the years, the report likened it to a 'story of old

LEFT: **The front anti-roll bar can be seen on this early TR6. On later cars, a small air deflector was fitted below the front valance.**

BELOW: **TR6s were available in a wide range of colours with changes made in line with the fashion of the day. Reds and blues were always popular.**

wine in new bottles, followed by new wine in the old bottle', finishing with the thought that the latest TR might be 'a new bottle holding contents which are very much in their prime', 'the best yet'. As the testers reported: '[We] drank our fill and enjoyed it.'

The body design met with general approval. *Autocar* noted that Karmann had provided a 'kind of smoothed-out TR with fashionable and effective use of matt black for the radiator grille and undercut tail panel'. *Autocar*'s writers were less complimentary about the handling, considering that the balance had been moved too far to understeer. Despite this, and a price that was ever-increasing (although the list price at just over £1,300 including purchase tax was described as realistic), the new TR6 was deemed to be 'one of the best fun cars around right now'. The article concluded with the thought that 'to go quicker is going to cost several hundred

Brighter colours were in vogue during the 1970s, with Magenta being one of the more striking colours available. Yellows and browns were also included among the options.

The final TR6 rolled off the production line in July 1976. Its revised bumper and front lamps, rubber over-riders and red-lined tyres identify it as a car that was destined for the United States. In time-honoured fashion, the assembly workers grouped around the car for a last TR6 picture.

© BMIHT

pounds more at least, so for performance alone the price is a competitive one. For the few joys of motoring left, it is a bargain.'

Writing in *Autosport* in July 1970, John Bolster commented that the car understeered too much when entering a bend at 110mph, comparing the poise of the TR unfavourably with that of a Triumph 2.5PI saloon. Bolster's view was that the TR was well suited to long-distance touring, 'while the power and flexibility of the engine look after rapid overtaking or

traffic crawling'. The failure of a drive shaft universal joint during acceleration tests, excused on the premise of press cars having an exceptionally hard life, gave an opportunity for both a convertible and hard-topped car to be tested. The team could not decide which was better, but they were convinced none the less that the TR6 was 'a real sports car of exceptional luxury'.

In the United States, the press reception was balanced. In February 1969, *Road & Track* expressed the opinion that

A TR PR DISASTER, PART ONE

At the end of 1972, Clive Richardson, then Deputy Editor of the renowned *Motor Sport* magazine, ordered a TR6 PI as his new company car. It was registered PGN 769L and delivered in February 1973. Despite the supplying dealer being aware of the profession of the purchaser, the car was delivered in an appalling condition, without even having been subject to the normal pre-delivery inspection. Despite his colleagues suggesting alternative products, including the Jensen-Healey and Morgan Plus-8, Richardson had chosen the TR on the basis of the fact that it had been in production through several iterations since 1952 and therefore ample time had passed to allow for any design defects to have been overcome – the reliability of the car should have been at its zenith. This was not to be the case. Instead, the car was delivered with 'so many faults that it might well have been the first car off the production line of a new model'. The new owner was not impressed, and made his views

quite clear in *Motor Sport* in November 1973: 'Its general finish was appalling, mechanically it was dreadful, and it was to be another 5500 miles before this Lucas fuel-injected motor car was to run consistently on six cylinders.'

Space in *Motor Sport* did not permit a complete list of the car's faults on delivery, but the writer did mention in that first piece the squeaking brakes, the misalignment of the doors, rust on the bodywork and hard top, paint spillage on the carpets and defective electrical components. And further items would come to light in subsequent articles during Richardson's ownership of the car, with a cracked cylinder head and a gearbox failure at 15,000 miles being the most serious.

The articles in *Motor Sport* generated the largest postbag received from readers of the magazine, nearly all recounting similar problems with new Triumph cars.

the changes represented 'one of those rare facelift jobs that actually comes off well. From the side, the car looks much the same as before.' Performance was no different from that of the outgoing TR 250 model, with just 104bhp being developed from the engine, but the view of *Road & Track* was that 'the engine [was] so smooth and quiet and so tractable at any speed, that you almost wouldn't know it was there if it weren't for a healthy note from the exhaust'. They also commented on the omission of petrol injection, noting that, while other manufacturers were incorporating fuel injection in order to meet emissions regulations, the new TR6 and the TR 250 that had preceded it had resorted to twin carburettors to satisfy the clean-air requirements and still deliver reasonable performance. Expectations for suspension had changed since the introduction of the TR4A four

years earlier, which had been subjected to some negative comments. The reviewer made mention of the chassis frame sitting underneath the axle, restricting suspension rebound, yet clearly the semi-trailing arm suspension arrangement of all TR 250s and TR6s sold anywhere in the world could not possibly have this restriction. Pricing in the US markets was appealing, at around $3,500, but there was a thought that, if Triumph were to develop an all-new car, perhaps to be called the TR7 it would 'probably be too good to be true' and the 'price would shoot way up'.

Nevertheless, the TR6 was to be the best-selling of all TR models by the time it went out of production. At the same time, production of the separate-chassis TR ended. Total production of all TR6 models was close to 95,000 cars, of which just under 8,400 were for the UK market.

CHAPTER EIGHT

HARRIS MANN'S WEDGE – THE TR7 AND TR8

TR goes back to its origins: a 2-litre, 4-cylinder engine with solid rear axle, although this was not how it was seen by all. Triumph comes up with a new engine design – the 'slant-four' – but fails to offer a convertible originally. The car is built initially on Merseyside at Speke, then at Canley and finally at the Rover plant in Solihull. Power enhancements with the Rover V8 engine give the motorist the TR8 and there are plans to fit the 16-valve 'Sprint' engine.

During the evolution of the car that was to replace the TR6, the organization that had now become British Leyland found itself in complete turmoil. Internal commercial complications between the former Nuffield and Austin companies had led to a situation in which a single town might have both Morris and Austin dealerships selling nominally identical cars in competition with one another. It had become even more complicated now, with Triumph, MG and Jaguar all competing in the same marketplace, yet being part of the same business. Engineering genius Harry Webster had been moved to the volume car business of Austin-Morris to sort out future product engineering difficulties. Spen King had been transferred from Rover to take his place and had been appointed Technical Director for Triumph. Clearly, some form of model consolidation would make sense.

In the sports-car market the management was faced with a serious problem, in that both MG and Triumph were supported by a loyal band of customers, who would not appreciate 'their' brand being sidelined in favour of the other. It is a friendly rivalry that continues today. Furthermore, the technology underpinning both the flagship Triumph TR product and the MG-B was from a different era and the market would be expecting something more modern, better suited to the late 1970s and 1980s.

In the end, the decision was taken to offer a single-model new sports car. The Triumph marque was to prevail, giving British Leyland a rational two-model strategy, with the Jaguar E-Type at the top of the range (at least until its replacement) and the TR as the more attainable product. The resulting car, known as the TR7, was to prove to be something completely different from anything that had been seen before; to many people, it was a striking and modern design, but to others it was an abomination. While earlier TRs had provoked comment for a slow rate of change, the new wedge-style TR came in for vociferous criticism for too much change too quickly.

MARKET REQUIREMENTS

During the period that led up to the birth of the new TR, mid-engined racing cars were achieving considerable success in all spheres of competition. Within the Leyland organization there existed considerable expertise in transverse-engine technology, although of course with the engine positioned at the front of the vehicle. With some considerable thought to the future, a decision was made to embark on two separate design studies – one at MG to consider a mid-engined layout and the other at Triumph to consider a conventional front-engined, rear-wheel-drive configuration. Triumph had some experience with front-wheel drive cars in the form of the 1300 and 1500, but these had longitudinally mounted engines.

Recognizing the continued importance of the US market, in late 1970 Mike Carver, from the product-planning

An original four-speed Speke-built car that has retained all its original features.

department, accompanied Spen King on a trip across the Atlantic. The aim was to gather the opinion of dealers, potential customers and selected motoring journalists to determine exactly what features would fit the needs of the market.

In many respects, their findings confirmed that the situation in this strategically important market was very similar to that which had presented itself in the early 1960s. It strongly favoured a low-cost and technically straightforward car. That appeared to rule out the MG design concept, with its transverse mid-engine and hydrolastic suspension. Price was, naturally, a significant factor. Ideally, it should be below that of the Datsun 240Z coupé, a car that was establishing a strong following in the USA, and the VW-Porsche 914.

As a result of all Carver and King's research, it was the Triumph study that was chosen as the basis on which the new car, to be code-named 'Bullet', was to be designed.

FEDERAL REQUIREMENTS

The 1965 book *Unsafe at Any Speed* (Grossmann Publishers, 1965), written by Ralph Nader, had helped to raise awareness of vehicle-safety issues in the United States, leading to a series of regulations to enforce the application of both passive and active safety requirements in motor vehicles. Some of these, such as low-speed-crash absorbing over-riders and door side-impact bars were already mandated and had been incorporated into earlier models for the US market.

Triumph's product planners were of the opinion that proposed Federal legislation would effectively outlaw convertible cars. It seemed clear that only a fixed-head monocoque construction could provide the required level of crashworthiness and side-impact protection. It was a view that was widely held at the time and the contemporaneously designed Jaguar XJ-S was also to emerge as a fixed-head coupé.

ADO21 – WHAT MIGHT HAVE BEEN

The MG design study was given the designation 'ADO21' and took a different approach from the Triumph version. The initial intention was to develop a replacement for the MGB, but, where the current MG was a conventional and simple car, ADO21 was to be a leap into the future. It was designed by MG at Abingdon and intended to be built in that facility, although costs would have been huge. The assembly lines at Abingdon, to the extent that they existed at all, would need to be totally rebuilt. No convertible version of ADO21 was considered. It was planned as a mid- or rear-engined car, on underpinnings that were taken from the Austin Maxi. Suspension would have been a sophisticated hydrolastic or hydragas semi-independent system and power was to be supplied by a BL 'E' series engine in a range of 1500cc or 1750cc but with the option of incorporating the E6 engine of 2227cc capacity. With its Abingdon design heritage, the car would naturally have been badged as an MG, with the idea of a possible Triumph version – similarly, there were a number of MG-badged TR7 designs.

At the time, a large engine plant had been built at Crofton Hackett near to the major Austin plant at Longbridge, with the intention of building 5,000 engines a week, some of which would find their way into ADO21. In fact, the predictions for engine supply proved to be wildly optimistic and the factory never reached its operating potential, although ADO21 might have provided a further outlet for the engine range.

No metal car was ever completed, although a conceptually similar car in the form of the FIAT X1/9 came on to the market in 1972. The general structure and layout of ADO21, although now as a convertible, using saloon-car underpinnings with a mid-engine format, eventually came to market much later as the MG F.

ENGINE, TRANSMISSION AND SUSPENSION

Earlier TRs had drawn their engine and transmission technology initially from Standard and latterly from Triumph saloon cars and this was to be continued with 'Bullet'. Rather than continue with the straight-six engine of the TR5 and TR6, which was becoming rather old in terms of its basic design and had gained a poor public reputation as a result of malfunctioning petrol-injection systems, Triumph would source the engine from the new Dolomite. In keeping with current trends, this engine was designed as a slant engine, which allowed a car to be designed with a low bonnet line.

There were thoughts about a higher-performance version of the car, ultimately destined to be launched as the short-lived TR8, and provision was also made to install a V8 engine. Two V8 engines were already available within the corporation: the in-house-designed 3-litre, overhead-cam design that was in principle two slant-four engines joined together, and the 3500cc engine, which had been used in the Rover P6B and was soon to find its way into the new Rover 3500. The

Triumph engine was experiencing a high level of warranty claims at the time, so it is hardly surprising that Spen King chose the Rover engine, especially given his background at Rover.

Between the two engines, there also existed an interesting higher-performance option in the form of the 16-valve overhead cam version of the 4-cylinder engine as used in the Dolomite Sprint. Characteristically for a Triumph, this had represented another industry 'first' in its implementation of a 16-valve engine in a 4-cylinder volume production car. Indeed, the novel design of the method by which the valves were operated, by a single camshaft, was to win an industry award for Triumph. While the V8-engined cars did eventually go into production, the 16-valve TR7, intended to be sold as TR7 Sprint, did not – at least not officially, even though a few pre-production cars have escaped and survived.

The original four-speed gearbox was developed from that used in the Morris Marina. The idea behind the suspension design was that it would have commonality with the car that was due to replace the Dolomite range. Front suspension was by MacPherson struts, and the rear suspension, in a complete break with the tradition established

TR7s were fitted with the Triumph slant-four engine with a capacity of 2 litres. Its low overall height allowed for a tidy installation under the low bonnet of the TR7.

In the TR8, the Rover-sourced V8 engine was a tighter fit.

ROVER, TRIUMPH AND THE SPECIALIST DIVISION

Rover and Triumph had always been competitors in the executive car market, and this was even more the case since the introduction of their respective 2000 models in 1963. Product rationalization within BLMC saw Rover and Triumph form the nucleus of what was called the 'Specialist Car Division' wherein two designs were to be developed, given the code names 'SD1' and 'SD2'. SD1 was destined to replace the Rover P6 and Triumph 2000/2500 model range. It was launched initially as the Rover 3500, with smaller engines of 2600cc and 2300cc, based on the Triumph straight-six engine but adapted to incorporate an overhead cam. SD2 was a stillborn concept intended as a replacement for the Dolomite range, using the slant-four engine and suspension from the TR7.

with the TR4A, reverted to a beam axle with coil springs, located with trailing arms. This seemingly retrograde feature is attributable directly to Spen King, who firmly believed that a well-designed beam-axle suspension would always be superior to an indifferent fully independent rear suspension.

CONTROVERSIAL BODY STYLE

As ever, the approval of the design of the car was a matter for senior management. With the Triumph proposal winning out over that offered by MG, and based on previous successful designs, it was no surprise that the hand of Giovanni Michelotti would be involved initially. For

once, however, perhaps because of a change in the balance of the top tier of management, the Italian maestro's work did not meet with unqualified enthusiasm. Instead, it was the Austin-Morris styling department, in the form of designer Harris Mann, that produced a design that could be approved.

Harris Mann had arrived at Leyland from the Ford Motor Company, where he had been involved in projects as different as the Capri and the D-series truck, and had evolved a contemporary, wedge-shaped style. Of Mann's three major designs for Leyland, the TR7 was to remain the purest representation of this style. Very few changes were made between the original design and the production version. All connection with the previous TR styling was abandoned, but, with the futuristic wedge-shaped profile, a commonality with the Austin-Morris product family emerged.

ABOVE: **Harris Mann's sketch design for the Leyland corporate sports car that became the TR7. A strong force behind the adoption of 'wedge' designs, the TR7 became the least modified and purest of all Mann's designs for British Leyland.**
© BMIHT

RIGHT: **Harris Mann, designer of the TR7, stands alongside a late-model TR7 coupé.**

ANOTHER STYLIST'S THOUGHTS

With its dramatic styling, the TR7 was bound to provoke comment from other designers. Perhaps the best-known, most biting remark was heard at the 1975 Geneva Motor Show, when Italian designer Giorgetto Giugiaro paused at the Triumph stand to consider the features of the new car. It was common practice to create an early clay model of a new car, incorporating a different design approach on each side, to allow consideration of both. Apparently, Giugiaro looked with great interest at one profile of the TR7, then moved around to turn his attention to the other profile, before exclaiming, 'They've done it to the other side as well!' Clearly, he was not impressed and his comment at the time was thought to sum up the views of many.

The distinctive wedge profile and scalloped swage lines along the sides of the car are obvious in views of the car from the rear three-quarter angle.

BUILDING THE TR7

The first off-the-tools TR7s were assembled during the summer months of 1974, with volume production ramping up through the autumn in time for a January 1975 launch, initially in left-hand-drive form and with all production destined for the United States. In another departure from TR tradition, the cars were to be assembled at Speke on Merseyside, which had previously assembled body shells for TRs that were transported to Canley for final assembly. Conversely, with TR7 assembly at Speke, engines, gearboxes and other major assemblies were transported northwards from the Midlands. With TR6 production still ongoing, the haulage industry was kept busy, transporting assemblies back and forth between the two major plants. Deliveries for the home market and the rest of the world were promised for the latter part of 1975, but UK deliveries in the end did not commence until the late spring of 1976.

The early cars offered only a four-speed manual gearbox without the option of overdrive, another TR feature with its origins in the earliest cars. Perhaps this was in keeping with the current market, where the introduction of five-speed overdriven gearboxes meant that overdrive was becoming an anachronism, but it was not an option on the TR7 until late 1976. A suitable overdrive unit was available as an option on the Dolomite 1850 and could easily have been engineered to be transferred into the TR, but this was never offered, although it was fitted to the competition cars. As a result, the early TR7 cars were under-geared and lacked the relaxed high-speed cruising style of their predecessors.

Triumph TR7 – Original North American Federal Specification

Layout and Chassis
Two-seat monocoque sports car

Engine
Type	Triumph slant-four in-line
Block material	Cast iron
Head material	Cast aluminium
Cylinders	4 in-line
Cooling	Water
Bore and stroke	90.3mm bore, 78mm stroke
Capacity	1998cc
Valves	2 valves per cylinder single overhead cam
Compression ratio	8.0:1
Fuel supply	2 Zenith-Stromberg 175CD2SEV carburettors
Max. power	92bhp @ 5,000rpm
Max. torque	115lb ft @ 3,500rpm
Fuel capacity	14.5 US gallons (55 litres)

Transmission
Clutch	Single dry plate, hydraulic actuation
Gearbox	BLMC 4-speed with synchromesh on all forward speeds

Ratios
1st	2.649:1
2nd	1.78:1
3rd	1.254:1
4th	1.00:1
Reverse	3.22:1
Final drive	3.63:1

Suspension and Steering
Front	Independent using MacPherson struts, anti-roll bar
Rear	Live axle, coil springs, radius arms, telescopic dampers, anti-roll bar
Steering	Rack and pinion
Tyres	175R70 13in or 185R70 13in
Wheels	Pressed-steel disc, or optional light alloy disc
Rim width	5.5 inches

Brakes
Type	Front discs, rear drums
Size	Front: 9.7 inches diameter / Rear: 8.0 x 1.5 inches

Dimensions
Track	
Front	55.5 inches (1,410mm)
Rear	55.5 inches (1,410mm)
Wheelbase	85 inches (2,160mm)
Overall length	164.5 inches (4,180mm)
Overall width	66 inches (1,680mm)
Overall height	50 inches (1,270mm)
Unladen weight	2,241lb (1,016kg), basic model increasing to 2,355lb (1,068kg), depending on options fitted

Performance
Top speed	109mph (175km/h)
0–60mph	9.8 seconds

Triumph TR7 – Non US Federal Specification

As US Federal version except as noted:

Engine
Compression ratio	9.25:1
Carburettors	2 SU HS6
Max. power	105bhp @ 5,500rpm (DIN)
Max. torque	119lb ft @ 3,500rpm

Dimensions
Overall length	160 inches (4,060mm)
Unladen weight	2,205lb (1,000kg) basic model, increasing to 2,356lb (1,068kg), depending on options fitted

ABOVE LEFT: **The original TR7 sales brochure included this cutaway drawing of the new car. Various interior features were changed for production cars, notably the substitution of the Dolomite-style nylon seat covers with the brighter tartan trim.** © BMIHT

ABOVE RIGHT: **The cockpit of the TR7 is a comfortable place to be, with ample leg and elbow room and comfortable seating.**

ABOVE LEFT: **The tartan trim even extended to the door cards.**

ABOVE RIGHT: **TR7s and TR8s utilized a modern dashboard, moulded as a single unit and presenting a totally different appearance to the earlier style used in the previous TR models. Use was made of printed wiring assemblies, but with mixed success, as poor solder joints and water ingress made for unreliability as the cars aged.**

RIGHT: **The boot was a decent size for a sports car, allowing ample space for a couple of suitcases. Stowage space inside the cockpit was more limited, as the space behind the front seats in earlier TRs was now missing.**

PRESS REACTIONS – THE EARLY TR7

In building a car that was in so many ways designed for the US market, Triumph had lost at a stroke the marketing advantage of the 'traditional British sports car'. The journalists assembled at Boca Raton, Florida, for the car's launch were well aware of this and a number of them commented on the car's 'stubby shape'. The influential magazine *Car & Driver* featured the TR7 on the cover of its April 1975 edition, describing the car as 'a major triumph'. *Road & Track* had intended to carry out extensive testing, but their initial report summed up the dire state of the Leyland Company at that time: 'We had hoped to have a full test of the TR7...but a strike in England prevented British Leyland from starting production and the cars shown were pilot models.'

John Dinkel, writing in the same magazine, noted that the new car was revolution rather than evolution from the TR6 model. In common with other writers, he mentioned the fact that the front of the car could not be seen from the driving position but he also commented favourably on the comfort of the cockpit. He compared the Triumph to the Datsun 240Z, a car that was selling well in the USA, and concluded that, at $5,100, it represented good value. According to Dinkel's colleagues Paul Frere and Ron Wakefield, the TR7 was the 'most important new British sports car in fourteen years' – the previous holder of that title was generally considered to have been the Jaguar E-Type, introduced in 1961.

A year later, the car went on sale in Europe and European journalists were able to report on the rest-of-world car, with its additional 15bhp. Without the Federal-specification mandated bumpers, the cars under test were slightly shorter and lighter. None of the reviews was completely fresh as all the writers had some experience of the US models. As usual, *Motor* and *Autocar* were to lead the reviews. *Motor* commented on the attractive interior and made special note of the instrumentation. Not surprisingly, the styling was described as 'startling', while the performance was 'reasonable', but visibility was poor and the gear change came in for adverse comment. One feature of the gearbox fitted to the TR7 was that it was very notchy when new and it could be difficult to engage the gears until it was well worn in. These reports were of course written at the time when the original four-speed gearbox was fitted, giving rise to a general consensus that the car was under-geared. Compared to the earlier TRs fitted with overdrive, this was undeniable.

Autocar reported similar impressions, although they did mention the car's North American targeting and determined that the maximum speed of 'only 109mph', and gearing 'such that the TR7 is uncomfortably fussy when cruising on a motorway at much over 70mph', may have been a result of the lower limits in North America. The writer had conveniently forgotten, perhaps, that the 70mph limit in the UK had been in existence for ten years at the time when the review was written. *Autocar's* review also emphasized that the new TR7 was not to be considered as a direct descendent of the earlier TR lineage: 'It is better to think of the TR7 as a two-seater version of the Dolomite'. Overall, the handling of the new car was praised – 'whatever else the old TRs might have done, they didn't go round corners all that well' – and the new simple beam-axle design was deemed to beat its predecessors 'hands down' in terms of that handling. The TR7, they concluded, 'is a long way from the rough ride standards of old-fashioned sports cars', which was, according to them, 'a tradition that deserve[d] to be broken'.

CHANGING GEARS

From late 1976, an automatic transmission was added to the options list for the TR7. It was never a popular option, not even in North American markets, but the new five-speed manual gearbox that was announced at the same time was a welcome addition. This had been developed in conjunction with the Rover 3500 car (otherwise known as SD1) and, when fitted to the TR, also included a revised and more robust rear axle, again derived from that fitted to the new Rover. With an eye to the North American market, the new five-speed box became a standard fitting, resulting in inadequate supply numbers being available for the rest of the world. With some embarrassment, in a situation that was becoming increasingly common within the hard-pressed British Leyland empire, the option was rapidly removed for other markets from the beginning of 1977. The company was not in a position to reinstate it until the following year, when it became a standard fit.

INDUSTRIAL UNREST

During the mid- to late 1970s, British Leyland continued to stumble from crisis to crisis. With hugely overlapping dealer networks, historic management scores to be settled and a militant industrial environment, it was perhaps too big to succeed, even in a perfect world. To make matters worse, the oil crisis of the early 1970s and ensuing financial melt-down affected all motor manufacturers. BLMC rapidly ran out of cash, necessitating a government rescue in 1975 – in everything but name, it was a nationalization. As owners of the business, the government then invited Lord Ryder, the renowned industrialist and Chairman of the National Enter-prise Board, to report on a restructuring plan. As far as TR production was concerned, his advice led to a closer integra-tion of the specialist division of Rover and Triumph into the volume car business, and the emergence of something called 'Leyland Cars'.

Ryder's strategy to 'rescue' Leyland did not work. Product rationalization and integration failed to create the hoped-for profits. The morale of the workforce dropped, with the con-tinuing fear of redundancy hanging over complete factories, and this led to a decline in quality. Warranty claims grew in number, labour disputes increased dramatically and manage-ment came and went, perhaps as a side effect of the even higher profile bestowed upon the company as a result of being publicly owned.

On 1 November 1977, the workforce at Speke went on strike, the same day as new group chairman Sir Michael Edwardes took office. With TR7 production completely stopped, the workforce may have anticipated a speedy

resolution to their grievances. Edwardes, however, had been appointed to restore some semblance of economic reality to the organization. With more important matters to attend to at the time, he was in no mood to capitulate to the work-force at Speke.

The strike at Speke continued over Christmas of 1977. In February 1978, the BL board took the decision to close the plant entirely. The strike was not the only issue lead-ing to the closure; the group had massive over-capacity and the Speke plant had been under consideration for closure even prior to Edwardes' appointment. The cars that were being produced were selling at a financial loss to the company, so it might have made commercial sense for the line to have been killed off, bringing an end to the TR story. Instead, the view was taken that the car helped to promote the entire product range in North America and thus supported the dealer network in that critical market. Provided that the losses could be stemmed, or at least reduced and contained, it was decided that produc-tion should continue. The line was moved to the home of Triumph at Canley.

Observers at the time considered that the rest of the BL workforce would not tolerate the closure of the Speke plant and that they would walk out in sympathy. However, perhaps sensing the inevitable, the Speke workforce accepted the clo-sure plans. The final TR7 to be built in Speke was completed

One of the victims of the closure at Speke was the planned TR7 Sprint, which would have used the 16-valve engine originally fitted in the Dolomite Sprint car. Although pre-production models were built, the car was never put on sale to the public. A number of genuine Sprint cars did manage to escape destruction and are now highly sought after.

LEFT: **Canley-built TR7s can be easily identified by the changed logo at the front of the car, now a Triumph laurel. This car, finished in Persian Aqua metallic paint, has the desirable full-length sunroof fitted.**

BELOW LEFT: **The move to Solihull brought yet another badge change. The last cars were fitted with a proper badge rather than a vinyl sticker.**

in May 1978 and the production facilities were installed at Canley, with body pressings being made by Pressed Steel Fisher at Swindon. The first TR7s left the Canley production line just five months later.

Canley would not be the final home of TR production. A further rationalization plan determined that the massive production facility at Canley, which had been constructed as recently as 1960, would cease production and all Rover and Triumph cars would be built at the Rover factory in Solihull. Production began in Solihull in April 1980, but the

final cars to be produced at Canley were not completed until August. Fourteen months later, all TR production would cease.

TR7 LOSES ITS HEAD

As the 1970s progressed, it became clear that the fear that US legislation would outlaw convertible cars was unfounded. The design studio of Giovanni Michelotti returned to the TR story, as BL looked to Italy again to transform the coupé into a convertible. A complete car was shipped to Turin and converted, with a very pleasing result. It looked almost as though it had been planned from the initial design and did not give the impression of being something of an afterthought.

Ten pilot cars were built at Speke during April and May 1978, in the aftermath of the bitter industrial dispute and amid the turmoil of the relocation to Canley. Unsurprisingly, volume production was then delayed and did not begin again until a year later. The convertible became available in the USA during the summer of 1979, appeared in early 1980 at the Brussels Motor Show, and finally went on general sale in March 1980 as the TR7 Drophead.

With the arrival of the convertible, the sales brochure began to show both styles of car, with the newest model being illustrated by way of a cutaway drawing.
© BMIHT

Little was to change in the cockpit of the convertible TR7, including the controls for the heater, which met with general approval.

The motoring press took the collective view that the open-top TR7 was the car that should have been launched in the first place. *Road & Track*'s Thomas Bryant wrote: 'It simply looks right – it's what the car should have been all along, with a clean crisp shape that evokes notions of speed and sports car driving excitement.' *Autocar* published a report in March 1980, with the view that the car was 'a changed and greatly improved concept for BL's sporting two-seater' and heaping praise on the new five-speed gearbox, which much improved the car's cruising ability: '[It was] a joy to drive along in winter with the hood down and with a generous supply of warm air from the TR7's very competent heater.'

LIVING WITH A TR7 CONVERTIBLE

Some owners are drawn into classic-car ownership via the most unlikely of routes. David Reeve took early retirement from a career in computers, most recently involved in UK air-traffic control systems, and set up a consultancy practice. One project came with an interesting catch: his commissioning client had an interest in classic cars and securing the deal involved David purchasing a convertible TR7, which he still owns. The car, built at Solihull towards the end of production and first registered in 1982, has been enhanced with a subtle body kit and a respray in a pale blue

Below the waistline the distinctive features of the TR7 remained, but the car took on an entirely new appearance. This example has its bumpers painted in body colour and is fitted with a subtle body kit.

metallic finish, believed to be a Mercedes-Benz colour. It suits the car well. The brakes have been improved, with four-pot callipers fitted to the front and a larger servo, providing braking performance comparable to a modern vehicle and giving the driver more confidence.

David does most of the maintenance work on the car himself, having honed his spanner skills, like so many, on 1960s and 1970s Fords. 'A lot of the design is very clever', he comments, 'but nothing is easy.' For example, replacing

the water pump required a special tool, a large screwdriver pressed into service as a lever and a hydraulic jack on top of the engine: 'Compare that to a Ford, where two or three bolts allow the water pump to just drop off the front of the block.' Like many other owners, he finds the visibility of the front corners difficult, making parking and close-quarter manoeuvring in confined spaces a challenge. On the other hand, he adds that the car is as comfortable on journeys of any length as either of his modern cars.

V8 ENGINES: THE TR8

It was always envisaged that the new car range would include a version using the 3.5-litre V8 Rover engine. The first announcement of such a car came from British Leyland's motorsport department, headquartered at the home of MG in Abingdon, Oxfordshire. They arranged homologation of a car called the 'TR7-V8' on 1 April 1978, by convincing the authorities that 400 such cars had been assembled.

In July 1979, the TR8 was officially launched in the USA, initially as a coupé but with convertibles being available from the third quarter of that year. A pre-production batch of TR8s had been built at Speke in 1977, but the long strike and the upheaval of moving production to the Midlands delayed the introduction. An additional bonnet bulge was needed to accommodate the V8 engine and, in the interest of product simplification, this bonnet style was also fitted to cars fitted with the slant-four engine. Apart from different badging and wider tyres fitted to alloy wheels, visually the car was identical to the TR7.

At first glance it could be a TR7, but in reality it is a rare and genuine right-hand-drive TR8 that was used for development work.

Triumph TR8 – Original North American Federal Specification

Layout and Chassis
Two-seat monocoque sports car

Engine

Type	Rover V8 (originally developed from Buick V8)
Block material	Cast aluminium
Head material	Cast aluminium
Cylinders	8 in 90-degree V formation
Cooling	Water
Bore and stroke	88.9mm bore, 71.1mm stroke
Capacity	3528cc
Valves	2 valves per cylinder, overhead valve
Compression ratio	8.1:1
Fuel supply	2 Zenith-Stromberg 175CD2SET carburettors (for 1980 model year, except California models) Lucas–Bosch L-Jetronic fuel injection (CA 1980 model year; all markets for 1981)
Max. power	133bhp @ 5,000rpm 137bhp with fuel injection
Max. torque	174lb ft @ 3,000rpm 168lb ft @ 3,250rpm with fuel injection
Fuel capacity	14.5 US gallons (55 litres)

Transmission

Clutch	Single dry plate, hydraulic actuation
Gearbox	BL 5-speed with synchromesh on all forward speeds
Ratios	
1st	3.321:1
2nd	2.087:1
3rd	1.396:1
4th	1.00:1
5th	0.833:1 (0.79:1 for 1981 model year)
Reverse	3.428:1
Final drive	3.08:1

Automatic transmission (option)

Type	Borg-Warner type 65 epicyclic with torque convertor
Ratios	
1st	2.39:1
2nd	1.45:1
3rd	1.00:1
Reverse	2.09:1
Maximum torque convertor multiplication	1.9:1
Final drive	3.08:1

Suspension and Steering

Front	Independent using MacPherson struts, anti-roll bar
Rear	Live axle, coil springs, radius arms, telescopic dampers, anti-roll bar
Steering	Rack and pinion
Tyres	185R70 13in
Wheels	Light alloy
Rim width	5.5 inches

Brakes

Type	Front discs, rear drums
Size	Front: 9.7 inches diameter Rear: 9.0 inches x 1.5 inches

Dimensions

Track	Front: 55.5 inches (1,410mm) Rear: 55.5 inches (1,410mm)
Wheelbase	85 inches (2,160mm)
Overall length	164.5 inches (4,180mm)
Overall width	66 inches (1,680mm)
Overall height	50 inches (1,270mm)
Unladen weight	2,565lb (1,163kg)

Performance

Top speed	135mph (217km/h)
0–60mph	7.7 seconds

An original and unrestored US-market TR8 coupé shows little change from the earlier car, other than the padded centre to the steering wheel.

TR8 – WHAT THE PRESS THOUGHT

It was characteristic of the situation in which Leyland found themselves as the 1970s drew to a close that the TR8 was launched into a market that was rapidly moving away from V8-engined small- and mid-sized cars. Indeed, this viewpoint was summed up in the letters column of *Autocar* in July 1979. That same magazine took a UK-registered TR8 coupé for testing, handing the car over to former sports-car and Formula 1 driver John Miles (or more correctly, the Honourable John Miles). His report was not encouraging: the Rover V8 engine 'wheezed and struggled under the burden of its emission equipment' and the rev counter 'crawled round to 5500rpm'. 'Terribly soft suspension made the car feel uneasy. It wallowed a second or third time in sympathy to gentle undulations,' he wrote, and 'tyre squeal, lots of roll and noticeable pad knock off accompanied hard cornering.' It was Miles's conclusion that the demands of the American market had turned 'this potentially super sports car into just another floppy

handling and riding boulevardmobile'. He urged Triumph to make some changes: 'Please convert it back into a sports car… [with] wider wheels, P6 tyres, vented brakes, taut suspension and more power.'

In June 1980 a road test of a TR8 convertible in Californian specification was printed in *Road & Track*. These testers were more positively inclined to the Triumph. Their testing had involved both injected (Californian) and carburetted (Federal) specification cars, but they were unable to identify any difference in performance while driving, concluding that detailed measuring would be required to validate the difference of just 4bhp. A top speed of 120mph (190km/h) was measured, along with a 0–60mph time of 8.4 seconds, which they said put the car 'in an acceleration league populated for the most part by cars that cost more than the TR8'. Less impressive was the fuel consumption, at 15 miles per US gallon.

The suspension issues were mentioned again, with comment that the front was 'rather soft, diving sharply under braking' and that some axle tramp could be induced when cornering on bumpy surfaces. Overall, the conclusion was positive. It was agreed that the Triumph engineers had found a good compromise, although there was a hope that a stiffer suspension might be offered as a future option.

On a positive note, the report added that enthusiast drivers would be happy to know that a 'mass-produced, lusty-hearted convertible', which would 'outrun most every other sports sedan and sports car this side of $15,000', was available. 'Buyers had best get in line quickly,' they wrote, noting that just 2,500 TR8s would be built for the 1980 model year. Of those, 90 per cent would be convertibles; for the California market, only convertibles would be available.

TR PRODUCTION ENDS

External politics once again played against Triumph. Even as production was being moved to Canley, the global economy was suffering from the second oil price crisis in fewer than ten years. Consequently, the market in the United States for large-capacity V8-engined cars decreased dramatically. The market for the big-engined TR was non-existent almost before it had begun. None of the eighty-one TR8s (sixty-three coupés and eighteen convertibles) built for the UK market was officially sold as a new car, although some were factory registered and resold. In the end, the rise in the value of the pound against the US dollar seriously damaged any possibility of selling TRs in the USA for a profit. As Sir Michael Edwardes summed up in his autobiography, 'The currency shift painfully exposed how unprofitable both TR7 and MG were to make as each model had so many unique components that it was impossible to achieve economic scale of manufacture.'

When the end finally came, Car & Driver had some gloomy comments to make: 'The British sports car is dead. The last of the breed, the TR7 and TR8 sibling, have finally succumbed... [because] the bean counters couldn't tolerate a negative cash flow for ever.' The article concluded that the TR7 had been the best example of the 'soon to be extinct breed', a new design and one that had received several enhancements since introduction – something that had been seen as uncharacteristic for such a range of cars. It is easy to look back and conclude that, had the magazine readers bought the cars in greater numbers, had the industrial-relations environment not been so challenging and had the management dealt more robustly with the issues that had confronted the British motor industry from the 1950s until its effective demise, it might still be possible to purchase a new TR today.

ABOVE LEFT: **Once again, a change of logo design was implemented for the TR8, here on the bonnet ...**

ABOVE RIGHT: **... and here at the rear of the car. The red side marker lights were mandatory for the USA and also fitted to this particular UK-market car.**

A TR PR DISASTER, PART TWO

Having taken a hit in 1973 over a poor-quality TR6 supplied to the Deputy Editor of the magazine *Motor Sport*, British Leyland might have been expected to take care to ensure that any future cars supplied to influential magazine writers, as either long-term test cars or for their own use, were of the best possible quality and properly prepared for delivery. The sub-title for a cover-feature article in *Motor* published on 13 August 1977 suggests otherwise: 'Somewhere if you look hard, there's a respectable car trying to get out, if only all the faults and failures would let it.'

Early in the article, the writer wondered whether he may been have issued with a 'Monday-morning car'. The build-quality issues exhibited by the car included difficulty in setting the choke correctly from cold starts to allow the engine to run properly before fully warmed up; a gear-change that was very stiff and hard to use; various unexplained general noises from the car; and random changes in the car's handling – something that had been noted on other TR7s at the time. The reviewer did enjoy one aspect of the car; while negotiating a roundabout, it was 'chucked' through a hedge, resulting in a comment about the car being 'chuckable' but not necessarily 'catchable'. Within 12,000 miles, the bodywork was showing signs of corrosion, especially around the headlight pods, and the report makes numerous references to the helpfulness of the roadside breakdown services, in a side swipe at the car's lack of reliability. The writer concluded that the car was 'a lemon, to use a technical term' and that he was not alone in his opinion, judging 'by the amount of correspondence I receive… and most complaints echo my own'.

CHAPTER NINE

TR RETURNS TO RALLYING

*Between the end of the TR4 campaigns and the introduction of the TR7, Triumph sporting endeav-
ours had focused on the small-chassis Spitfire at Le Mans and in rallying, the large 2.5PI saloons
in endurance rallying and the smaller Dolomite saloons in rallying and saloon-car racing.*

The TR7, in 4-cylinder and latterly in V8 engine formats, her-
alded a significant return to motorsport for the TR range of
cars. Responsibility for competitions had moved to the MG
home at Abingdon and was now under the careful control of
Ron Elkins and Bill Price, both masters at interpretation of
the FIA homologation rules to provide the best advantage
for their teams.

The engineering of the rally cars began before the car
entered production, with work on what had been a production development car. Elkins and Price applied all their skill in
interpreting the rules, and their knowledge of suitable parts
and sub-assemblies available that could qualify for homologation, to pull together a specification for a car that, at least
on paper, looked to have competitive potential. The numerous production delays resulted in the homologation papers
being submitted some eighteen months before the car went
on sale and then only in the United States. The continuing
industrial turmoil affecting the Leyland Group contributed
to delays in supplying the cars and the special parts needed,
but three cars were eventually constructed. Of these, two
were to compete and the third was to be used as a test and
development tool, eventually to be the first competition car
to be fitted with the V8 engine.

FIRST EFFORTS

The two competition cars were powered by 16-valve Sprint
engines fuelled by two twin-choke Weber DCOE carburettors developing around 220bhp as compared with the road-

going car's 105bhp. Transmission was via a four-speed gearbox fitted with overdrive in the style of the Dolomite Sprint,
even though overdrive was never available as an option on
a factory-built car.

The two competition cars were registered KDU 497N
and KDU 498N and the test car was KDU 496N. A full
programme was constructed for the 1976 season, but early
events had to be cancelled, for no reason other than the fact
that the cars were not available. The first appearance was
to be on the Welsh Rally with the two cars driven by Brian
Culcheth and Tony Pond. Neither car was to finish this event.

By August 1976, the rear suspension had been modified
with the addition of a Panhard rod and the cars finally began
to complete events. Tony Pond took the podium twice in
1976, with third place in the Manx Trophy and first in the
Raylor Rally. Although the Raylor was a minor event, held
in the forests of North Yorkshire, a win was still a win, and
certainly significant in terms of publicity when it is the first
for a new type of car. The Manx Rally that year was the first
event in which both TR7s were to compete and finish, with
Brian Culcheth's car finishing in fifth place.

Just in time for the Lombard RAC Rally, held in November of 1976, two new cars were prepared. They were still
powered by Sprint engines, but by now the new five-speed
gearbox had replaced the earlier four-speed and overdrive.
The plan had been to fit the cars with all-round disc brakes.
This did not happen, although the successful Panhard rod-
style suspension was installed. Both cars were to suffer
rear-suspension failures during the RAC; Tony Pond's was
terminal and resulted in his retiring from the event. Earlier

Spen King, Bernard Jackman and Jim Parkinson examine the Design Council Award-winning Sprint engine cylinder head where a single camshaft was arranged to operate four valves per cylinder.
© BMIHT VIA NATIONAL MOTOR MUSEUM

Brian Culcheth inspects the build of his car for the 1976 rally season. The sliding switches for the vehicle's lights had been replaced with traditional toggle switches.
© BMIHT

One of the completed TR7
Sprint rally cars for the
1976 season. Although never
offered on production cars,
the toggle switch to operate
the overdrive is visible on the
gear stick.
© BMIHT

in the event, Pond had overcome damage caused to the steering by a fractured wheel becoming jammed in the rack and the inevitable accident that ensued. The wheel had in turn been damaged when the car hit a rock on the track during one of the stages in Kielder Forest. The second car, driven by Brian Culcheth and his long time co-driver Johnstone Syer, did finish, in ninth place. Problems included two rear-suspension failures and gearbox difficulties. The original gearbox lost all ratios except fourth and the replacement failed towards the end of the event, losing second gear and being unable to select bottom gear unless the car was stationary.

A NEW YEAR

The mixed bag of successes and failures continued in 1977. The year started with a win in Belgium in February for Tony Pond competing in the Boucles de Spa event at the wheel of KDU 497N. Leyland had appointed a new Director of Motorsport, John Davenport, who was to be closely associated in the future with the Metro 6R4 project. For 1977 his mission was to introduce a more formal and business-like regime to the works team. A review of the performance of the cars in the 1976 season had shown that the TR7's

strength was on tarmac. As a result, the 1977 programme included events where it was hoped that smoother surfaces would reflect the car's abilities better than the challenges that had been posed on the forest tracks of the previous year. Their hard work in reviewing the programme did pay off to some extent. As well as Pond's success in Spa, there was a second for him in the Scottish Rally and third places in both the Tour of Elba and Mintex.

Brian Culcheth came home second in the Manx Trophy, but it was an event that was not without controversy and may have contributed to Culcheth leaving the team at the end of the year. Prior to the event, testing of a revised suspension package for tarmac handling had taken place at Caldwell Park, which would have been ideally suited for the Manx event. However, when the new car, OOM 512R, was shipped to the Isle of Man, it soon became apparent that the package that had been developed and tested had not been fitted to the car. Nevertheless, despite further setbacks and mechanical failures, Culcheth set eight fastest stage times in achieving what was to be the best performance of a 4-cylinder TR7 in a British international event. The same car also competed in the RAC Rally at the end of the year, the final event that Culcheth was to drive for the Leyland team. He was forced to retire during the first day with broken wheel studs.

RIGHT: **Culcheth and Syer came home to a ninth overall place in the Scottish Rally in 1977. In the other team car, Tony Pond finished in second place to secure the manufacturers' team prize.**
© BMIHT

BELOW: **Driven by Brian Culcheth, OOM 512R competes in the 1977 Manx Rally in one of the best-ever motorsport performances of a four-cylinder TR7.**
© BMIHT

TR7 RALLY CAR RECOLLECTIONS – BRIAN CULCHETH

'I started with the TR7 in 1975 when I was asked to critique the car with a view to it being rallied. My report said that the suspension was too soft, there wasn't enough power and there wasn't enough space inside the car. I recall something about only just enough room for a lady's handbag! The shape of the car made forward visibility very difficult, which didn't help at all on forest stages when you really want to know where the corners of the car are. We'd had problems previously with the Sprint engines in the Dolomites with head gasket failures and it was really disappointing to have this again with the TR7. It took me out of the Welsh Rally in 1976 and Tony [Pond] had the same problem in the Scottish. Then in the RAC, I had a couple of gearbox problems. The replacement gearbox had no second gear and I couldn't get into first without completely stopping. So approaching Bath at the end of the event for some of the corners I had to come to a complete stop, change into first and drive off. I could sense the spectators thinking, "What's this fool playing at", or words to that effect.

'Then for the Manx in 1977, we'd been testing and found a rear anti-roll bar made a huge improvement to the handling on tarmac. My car turned up for the event without one fitted. I protested to [John] Davenport about this, but was told that it made no difference. In the end it was a case of drive the car as it was or quit the team there and then. Despite this, though, we got a good result. We tried a new clutch as an experiment. I said it was useless as it was prone to slipping, but was told it was needed for "testing purposes" and would not be replaced. We had a whole series of really silly failures – oil pipes falling off, wheel studs failing, the bodies flexed and on one occasion, I had the floor actually fall out.

'These cars had poor steering as well. You could go round the same turn six times without any problem, but on the seventh for no good reason, it would just run off the road. Especially when testing, there were sections of "off" that I got quite familiar with!

'1977 was a pretty disastrous year and I left the Leyland team at the end of the year. I never really felt that they had their heart in it.'

Brian Culcheth demonstrates the ability of a TR7 to manage on two wheels.
BRIAN CULCHETH

In the 1977 Tour de Corse, Culcheth and Syer were the highest-placed British team in the Sprint-engined TR7.
BRIAN CULCHETH

TR7 V8 – QUALIFIED SUCCESS

Testing of the rally-specification TR7 V8 had been ongoing for some time prior to the car's first outing in the 1978 season. Again, the homologation experts at Abingdon had been able to convince the authorities to sanction the V8-engined car for motorsport, despite it not going on general sale to the public until more than eighteen months into the future. With the departure of Brian Culcheth at the end of the previous season, Tony Pond remained as the sole top-flight driver. Fuel delivery to the engine was initially using dual twin-choke Weber carburettors; later iterations of the engine would use Pierburg fuel injection, although an installation of four Weber carburettors was also used. The target was to achieve a power output of 300bhp to compete with the contemporary Ford Escorts, which were offering around 250bhp.

Three outright wins were achieved in 1978, starting in Aberdeen, Scotland, with the Granite City Rally. This was a significant achievement since from 1968 onwards the event had been won outright by Fords (an Anglia in 1968 and Escorts in other years). Pond then went on to achieve suc-

cess with his co-driver Fred Gallagher in the 24 Hours of Ypres and the Manx Trophy. In the RAC Rally that year, they were to finish in fourth position, despite numerous mechanical failures seeing him in last place shortly after the event commenced.

In a replay of the situation that had developed the previous year, Pond had become unsettled within the team and was to leave for a seat in the following season driving for Chrysler. Before the RAC Rally, he took the same car to Corsica for the Tour de Corse, a tarmac event that should have suited the TR7 V8 nicely. Within hours of the start, the car was out of the event with a seized gearbox. It was found that the drain plug was loose; whether it was an unfortunate incident or a deliberate act of sabotage by a rival team was never established, but oddly enough the same fate befell the second TR7 V8 entered in the event and driven by Jean-Luc Therier.

Meanwhile, Brian Culcheth's old car, KDU 497N, had been reconstructed as a TR7 V8 and was campaigned in three rallies: Ulster, Manx Trophy and Cork. In each event, the car was withdrawn following mechanical failures – two engine-related incidents and a gearbox seizure. It also failed to proceed in its final appearance while competing in the Hitachi Rallysprint

OOM 514R was a long-serving works car, originally built with a 4-cylinder engine that was subsequently replaced with a V8. It was driven with success by Graham Elsmore in 1979. Now privately owned, the car is shown here in 'retirement' at a rally sprint event held at Goodwood.

because of electrical failures. For 1978, OOM 512R, the car in which Culcheth ended his Triumph career, had also been rebuilt with a V8 engine and repainted in a distinctive red and blue colour scheme. This was to be its final year. After Tony Pond's victory in Aberdeen and a successful drive in the televized Rallysprint competition, the car was shipped to Canada to compete in the Criterium de Quebec. When it returned, the car's final event as a works entry was to be the 1978 Wyedean Rally under the control of Graham Elsmore.

In 1979, there was a succession of retirements in National events, while two Scandinavian drivers, Per Eklund and Simo

Lampinen, were recruited for the European events, replacing Tony Pond. The highest-profile results that year came in the Mintex, with a second overall for Per Eklund, and a third place in the Manx Trophy for Graham Elsmore. Simo Lampinen won the TV Rallysprint event but was ruled out of time in the 1000 Lakes Rally held in his home country as a result of ignition failures. Eklund finished in eighth place.

Tony Pond was to return for 1980, along with Roger Clark, who joined after a long and successful career driving Ford Escorts. By lucky coincidence, Roger Clark's car-sales business had recently taken on a Leyland franchise and the

Again in private ownership, SJW 548S had some success in 1979 with Nordic drivers Simo Lampinen and Per Eklund. At this time, the cars were driven with the headlights in the up position, as much to help the driver judge the corner of the car as anything else, and with substantial additional driving lights added.

publicity for both parties was no doubt welcome. Pond was to achieve several successes in 1980, with the Manx Stages event held on closed public roads in May of that year showing what was to come later. In spectacular style, Pond not only achieved an overall win for his TR7 V8 but also set the fastest time on all but two of the fourteen special stages of the event. This success was to be repeated on the Isle of Man in September with a further outright win in the Manx Trophy. Per Ekland also achieved a creditable third place overall in the 1000 Lakes. The success in Rallysprint continued, showing that the TR7 V8 was an exceptionally fast car in a straight line, although the results card for events held on loose surfaces continued to show a litany of DNFs.

The chapter on TRs in factory-supported motorsport was heading inexorably to a close. Competition-car preparation continued at Abingdon, but the decision had been taken to cease production of MG cars and to sell the site for redevelopment. The entire future for the competitions department was questionable, to say the least.

The final works car was registered on 1 August 1980, with a new 'W' registration plate. It was to be crewed in

the Lombard RAC Rally in November by Tony Pond and his regular co-driver Fred Gallagher. Keeping Pond and Gallagher company in a three-car works team entry were Per Eklund and Hans Sylvan in a second TR7 and Roger Clark and Neil Wilson in a third. Pond's car was the only one of the three to finish the event, the other two being withdrawn with oil-related failures; Eklund's car suffered a deranged oil pump and Clark's car a failed oil pump. Pond was to finish in seventh place overall, having once again fought his way back through the field following an incident on the first stage at Longleat Safari Park, when his car left the track and was in collision with an animal feeding station. Time was lost rectifying body damage and fitting a new windscreen. A second incident, in Yorkshire, where the car again departed from its intended course, cost more time. Despite or perhaps because of the setbacks, Pond achieved top-three times on twenty-five of the sixty-seven special stages that were actually competed (with three having been cancelled), to achieve a final place of seventh overall.

And with that, the TR7 V8 programme came to a halt.

CHAPTER TEN

VARIATIONS ON A THEME

From the very earliest introduction of the TR2, the base structure of the car was used for the basis of other cars that competed with and complemented the output from Standard-Triumph. Whether it was new body styling, enhanced creature comforts or more space, a number of variations on the basic theme of the TR were available, some of which were to sell in respectable numbers.

IMPERIA FRANCORCHAMPS TR2

In the late 1940s, prior to establishing their own subsidiary assembly plant, Standard-Triumph had entered into an agreement with the Belgian Imperia Automobile company to assemble kits of parts into fully built-up cars, for sale in Europe. Located in the Ardennes town of Nessonvaux, Imperia had previously designed and built their own motor cars during the 1920s and 1930s, slowly absorbing other Belgian

An Imperia Francorchamps TR2 displayed in as-built condition. The green paint finish suits the car's style very well.

manufacturing concerns. One unusual feature of the factory was the vehicle test track located on the roof of the building, built in 1928 in the style of the facility at FIAT's Turin site dating from 1923. The infrastructure of Belgium had suffered badly from the ravages of the Second World War, and the simple fact that Imperia's was one of the very few industrial buildings to have survived was perhaps a strong deciding factor in Standard-Triumph's decision-making.

With a previous expertise in designing their own cars and coachwork for other chassis, Imperia were well placed to develop a new body design to exploit niche markets not addressed by the mainstream model. The result was the Francorchamps coupé. The main requirements for the coupé were improved weather protection and a more 'civilized' passenger environment, with the aim of moving the car into a more upmarket segment – rather like the Jaguar fixed-head coupé. To this end, the coachwork incorporated a fixed roof, the door tops were extended, with a gentle concave curved top, and the designer had included the luxury of both wind-up windows and locking doors. The rear of the roof featured a large window and the top was fitted with an opening Plexiglas section. During the manufacturing period, of just over a year, both long-door and short-door variants were built, the design being changed in accordance with the kits sent from Canley. In keeping with the market positioning, the interior finish included proper door cards, which restricted the amount of elbow room available inside, a heater and leather seats fitted as standard. Pricing was in keeping with the market position aspirations at around 50 per cent more than the base model TR2. Just twenty-two cars were assembled.

SWALLOW DORETTI

Origins

The paths of the Swallow Coachbuilding Company and the Standard Motor Company first crossed in the 1930s. Initially, Swallow's business had been the construction of sidecars for the booming motorcycle market before creating highly distinctive bodies built on the chassis of Austin Sevens and later creating similar designs on chassis sourced from Ford and Wolseley, among others. While the finished cars had a rakish and sporting appearance, their rather mundane underpinnings resulted in a somewhat pedestrian performance that did not match the styling. Company joint owner, William (later Sir William) Lyons, was keen to develop the business

further and to offer a car whose performance matched the expectations that arose from its appearance.

Negotiations with the Standard Motor Company were fruitful and a supply of engines and other components was arranged to form the basis of a new car, which first went on show at the 1931 London Motor Show. It was to be marketed under the brand 'SS'. Although it is fairly clear that one of the Ss in the company name probably stood for 'Swallow', the meaning of the second letter has been widely discussed, but it could refer to the significant contribution of Standard. Although sidecar construction continued, by 1933 the company had been retitled as 'SS Cars' and, shortly after, the sidecar business continued as the Swallow Coachbuilding Company. Following the Second World War, the connotations of the 'SS' title were such that Lyons felt that the company needed a new name, eventually deciding on 'Jaguar'. The sidecar business was sold as a going concern to Helliwells, based at Walsall Airport and subsequently acquired by the giant Tube Investments company.

In an attempt to compensate for the decline in the sales of sidecars, Swallow were building a small scooter, the Gadabout, designed by Frank Rainbow. Rainbow and Eric Sanders, then head of Helliwells, were to be pivotal to the Doretti story. Sanders, a friend of Sir John Black, was on a business trip to the United States and met with the Rome Cable Corporation of California, headed by Arthur Anderson. It was a business with similar interests and Anderson also had plans to import and sell the new TR2 in California, as well as a grand idea to develop a sports car that might fulfil the Californian Dream. It is a simple step to complete the connection between Sanders, Anderson, Rainbow and Black, with Swallow creating a car for Anderson to market in the USA, built on TR sub-assemblies and leveraging the experience of Tube Investments' expertise in tubular steel. Working with a team of just five, the car went from outline concept to finished prototype in nine months.

The Car

Built on a chrome-molybdenum steel tubular chassis, with raw materials supplied from within the TI group, the car was clothed in aluminium panels with steel doors and inner body shells front and rear bolted to the chassis. The chassis design was immensely strong, based on current practice for Grand Prix race cars, with the rear suspension utilizing radius arms to tame the tendency of the TR2 axle to tramp. Overall, the

THE ORIGINS OF A NAME

Dorothy Deen was born in Hollywood, California in 1922, the daughter of Arthur Anderson and wife Martha. From an early age it was apparent that her life was not to follow the typical route for the age, to becoming a Californian wife and mother. A motoring and racing enthusiast, she began by testing the motorcycles that her father had redesigned and went on to wholesale motoring accessories, with the sponsorship of her father's business interests and the skills of machine operator Paul Bernhardt. Dorothy's business was formerly named Cal Specialties but she soon embarked on a search for a more exciting brand name. Taking the first three letters of her own name and adding an Italian feel, she came up with the rather appealing 'Doretti'.

Doretti was an inch (2.5cm) longer than the TR2, but the chassis was 6 inches (15cm) longer and 3 inches (7.5cm) wider, giving a smoother ride. By mounting the engine slightly further back in the chassis, a near-perfect weight distribution was achieved, ensuring secure handling. Despite the increased dimensions, the interior space and boot space were smaller than those of the TR2.

The bodywork for the prototype and production cars was undertaken by Panelcraft Ltd locally in Birmingham and the bodies were then shipped to Wallsall for final assembly.

Mechanically, the engine, gearbox and rear axle were standard TR2 units; the instrument panel from the TR was also utilized, although the speedometer and rev counter were positioned either side of the central instrument cluster.

The aim of the styling was to make the car attractive to the target customer on the West Coast – an interesting blend of mid-1950s European sports car, with the appearance of a Ferrari from the front, particularly in terms of the radiator grille. From the rear, there were distinct similarities with the Austin Healey 100 and from the side, with the MG A.

Spotted at the TR Register International Rally, a Swallow Doretti displayed under ongoing restoration. At first glance, the grille gives the car the appearance of a Ferrari of the same era.

Another Doretti at a major car show event. The rear bumper is of the blade type often associated with this car and the side screens are in place.

The comfort of both driver and passenger was enhanced over the Triumph, with a heater fitted as standard – it remained as an option on the TR. The doors were full height, giving a better sense of security – with the Triumph's cutaway doors, both driver and passenger could have the feeling of their elbows scraping the tarmac if the driving was at all adventurous – and glazed panels replaced the side screens. As an added sophistication, whereas entering a TR2 with weather gear installed entailed opening a zip and reaching for a pull cord, the Doretti provided the owner with door levers. Prospective owners might expect to pay a premium for these additional comforts, and they did: against a list price of £910 for the TR2, the Doretti sold for £1,102, both prices being inclusive of tax.

A Sales Success?

The first car was shipped to New York on board the liner RMS *Queen Mary* in September 1953, accompanied by Frank

Rainbow. It was then transported by air to California, where it was shown in January 1954 alongside another car and chassis in the company of a number of TR2s. Dealers attended from the western United States and both the Doretti and TR2 were viewed with great enthusiasm. As might be expected for a launch in that particular location, numerous show-business personalities attended, giving a glamorous air to the event. The UK launch, a much lower-key event, involved a track day held at Silverstone to give the press an opportunity to test the car. Advertising appeared in the magazines in November 1954, offering cars for immediate delivery.

Production lasted for a short period, coming to an abrupt end just ten months later in 1955. It has been widely suggested that pressure was exerted on Tube Investments by other car builders who were its clients, and that the value of the component and raw material business was greater than that of the Swallow car. There was a concern that alternative sources to the many items bought in from

Swallow Dorettis wore this badge on the bonnet.

There could be no doubt about the make or model of the car with this descriptive badge affixed to the bonnet.

TI group companies would be found unless production ceased. In particular, it seems that, with supreme irony, Jaguar considered that the Doretti posed a threat to the success of its XK120.

A total of 275 cars were built. At the very end of production, two new cars were built to a revised design by Frank Rainbow that would have been sold as the Swallow Sabre, but it was not to be.

PEERLESS/WARWICK

Origins of the Name

Peerless as a vehicle business had its origins in the United States and came to prominence in the UK in the years following the Great War. It was during this conflict that the advantages of mechanized transport came to the fore and, following the Armistice, the market was awash with war surplus lorries. The Peerless Company of Cleveland, Ohio, had been a substantial supplier and ultimately gave its name to a business established in Slough, Berkshire, formally registered as 'Slough Lorries and Components Limited', to refurbish the surplus vehicles for future civilian use. The Peerless name continued to be used in the 1950s for a Jaguar dealer in the town, but was subsequently to be launched into manufacturing following a meeting at a hotel in the Midlands.

Origin of the Car

James 'Jimmy' Byrnes owned a restaurant called the Saxon Mill in the city of Warwick, just a few miles from Coventry. It was a favourite establishment of the board members of Standard-Triumph, who were frequent visitors. Byrnes was a keen motor-racing enthusiast and had ambitions to race a car built to his own specification. Bernie Rodger had a reputation in the mid-1950s as a tuner of racing engines and for the construction of 'specials' and it was to Rodger that Byrnes turned for help with his own project. In the way of such things, the project soon ventured off course, from a special racing car to a low-volume production sports GT car, where Rodger and Byrnes believed that commercial success might exist.

Jimmy Byrnes had established useful contacts at Triumph through his restaurant business and felt, rightly as it transpired, that Standard-Triumph might be a suitable supplier of component parts. Taking an engine, transmission and front suspension of the type used in the TR3, Bernie Rodger built a frame utilizing 1.5 × 1-inch 16-gauge rectangular-section steel tube and clothed it in a hand-crafted aluminium body. The car was extensively tested, producing impressive performance figures, with speeds around 120mph (190km/h) and a 0–60mph acceleration time of less than ten seconds.

The next stage was to seek the valued opinion of John Gordon, a former army colleague of Jimmy Byrne, a racing enthusiast and the owner of a Rolls-Royce dealership in Slough. Asked to give a view on the car's market suitability, he

A fully restored Peerless, showing the car's long and low profile well.

said that he felt it would sell better as a four-seated GT car in a 2+2 layout. This resulted in a number of changes, including a widening of the track, which allowed the rear suspension to be modified to incorporate a de Dion rear axle within the space frame. By doing this, they had beaten Triumph to an independent rear suspension design by some eight years.

Prototype number two was built, again in aluminium in a 2+2 seating layout, and shown to the public at the Paris Motor Show in 1957. With the full approval of the Standard-Triumph directors, preparations were made for the supply of sub-assemblies and production of the new car.

Production

Originally, the car was to be launched as the Warwick, recalling the city where the concept and design had originally been developed. However, following the receivership of the Jaguar dealer using the Peerless name, a facility in Slough became available, and the car became the Peerless 2-litre GT. The idea was to leverage the strength of the brand name and its familiarity in the United States, a primary market for the car. Prices and contracts were agreed with Standard-Triumph for components and a local manufacturing company in Slough was engaged to build the space frame and de Dion rear-axle tube. Luckily, the managing director of the company in Slough was another motoring enthusiast.

Continuing production of the cars in aluminium would have incurred tooling costs that would drive the price up too much for a car that was always envisaged as a low production model. Following discussions with British Resin Products Ltd, a subsidiary business of the mighty Distillers Company, it was decided to adopt instead the relatively new technology of Glass Reinforced Plastic. A search was carried out for a company that would be able to create the tooling for the moulds and thence to create the body. The ideal candidate was found in James Whitson Ltd, which had manufacturing facilities close by in West Drayton and expertise in constructing lightweight coachwork for motor coaches, particularly the distinctive observation one-and-a-half-deck coaches that were popular at the time, and in specialist vehicles for use in the developing air-transport business.

In the Market

The reception of the prototype during the Paris Motor Show led to expectations of production volumes that could exceed 1,500 cars per year. One US distributor requested an allocation of eighty cars per month and an option to increase this to 150 cars per month. In May 1958 the first production cars were displayed, enjoying a positive reception from the press. The October 1957 issue of *Motor Sport* carried a brief editorial – based on the specification of the second prototype, so suggesting that the coachwork would be in aluminium – reporting that the prototype was 'thrashed for 6,000 miles absolutely trouble-free'. In other reports, the car was described as 'the sports car for the family man'.

With a view to demonstrating the durability of the Peerless GT and the promotor's confidence in it, a car was entered at Le Mans for the 1958 24 Hours (see Chapter 4). The resultant boost to sales meant that the company soon needed new premises, and the production facilities were moved to the northern outskirts of Slough.

The Peerless used the same power unit as the TR3 and period model Morgan, but it offered higher performance than both, despite weighing more. This was partly because of the more streamlined shape and partly because of the more sophisticated rear suspension design, which almost completely eliminated wheel spin. With a wider track and longer wheelbase, the ride of the Peerless was better than that of the TR3, with body roll virtually eliminated. Naturally, this all came at a price: while a new TR3 could be obtained with change from £1,000, including purchase tax, Peerless was asking £1,490 for the GT car. Still, they had no difficulty in selling every car that could be made. Sales Manager Simon Hall has been reported as saying that he never actually needed to sell a car – interested parties simply took a short test drive and then immediately left a deposit to join the end of the list in an ever-increasing order book.

New Models

Despite the sales success of the GT, it was not without a few issues. Concerns had been raised about the quality of the GRP moulding and these appeared irresolvable with the

ABOVE LEFT: **A very simple frontal appearance, with the distinctive 'P' in the grille.**

ABOVE RIGHT: **Tail fins were still fashionable ornaments at the time when the Peerless was designed – they made for a distinctive detail to the rear of a car.**

Deeply sculptured rear seats provided plenty of storage space. Unlike many cars following the 2+2 layout, there was some leg room for adult rear-seat passengers. The large handle in the centre of the door card was used to lift and lower the window glass.

The TR origins of the instruments and steering wheel are still discernible.

Very clearly a Standard-Triumph wet-liner engine, here installed in a Peerless. The oil filler did not clear the low line of the bonnet and the asymmetric shape of the rocker cover made simply rotating the cover impossible, so the filler was relocated. Pre-dating the TR4, the bonnet needed a bulge to clear the carburettors.

incumbent supplier, leading to a subtly redesigned body and a revised production method undertaken by Wincanton Transport and Engineering. The revised car was launched on the market as the Peerless 2-litre GT Phase 2 in the summer of 1959. Perhaps the most significant change was the reduction in mouldings used for the newer design. Whereas the earlier design used no fewer than fifty-seven individual mouldings, which needed to be assembled and bonded to create the body shell, the new body was made as a single moulding. As well as reducing the weight of the body and increasing quality through reducing the number of assembly operations, the body shell was stronger and so less liable to flex. Detail changes included a simple grille, replacing the earlier ornate design that incorporated a distinctive letter 'P' at its centre, and, in response to comments from owners of earlier cars, the addition of stays to the doors to prevent them from damaging the bodywork.

With the introduction of the Phase 2 cars a sales visit to the United States was made following the shipping of the first two left-hand-drive finished cars – one to Detroit and the other to Los Angeles for the attention of none other than Dorothy ('Doretti') Deen.

Regretfully, a dispute among the directors occurred shortly after the announcement of the Phase 2 car, leading to the resignation of John Gordon and fellow director Sam Rostron. Their departure caused serious concern among the suppliers, worried that their invoices might not be paid. Peerless Motors, the sales arm of the organization, was stripped of its franchise and consequently fell back into receivership. Peerless Cars, the manufacturing business, met a similar fate, but its assets were liquidated and, with the enthusiasm of the remaining directors undiminished, a new company, Bernard Rodgers Developments Ltd, was incorporated.

The new business turned again to James Whitson for the manufacture of the bodywork, taking advantage of improvements in GRP technology that allowed for the body shell to be further lightened and yet for its strength to be increased. In a design feature that was to be seen in the future on the Jaguar E-Type, and had already been used by Triumph on the new Herald, the entire bonnet could be tipped forward and removed. This provided for much-improved access to the engine and front suspension.

The profile of the roof design was modernized, with gutters moulded above the cant rail level forming small fins on the roof and matching the fins on the rear wings. Internally, the instrument display was rearranged and placed centrally, to provide greater commonality between right-hand and left-hand-drive models. The new car was announced to the world as the Warwick 2-litre GT, finally being given the name that it had almost had in 1958, in recognition of its spiritual place of birth. With a list price of £1,666, it was faster than any other four-seater car for the money and *Motor* reported that it offered 'a distinctive combination of size, price and performance unique amongst British sports cars'.

Although the Warwick model was to continue in various forms into the 1960s, almost overlapping TR4 production, the TR story ends with the 2-litre car. Future developments focused on American V8 engines, until the final demise of the company in 1962, following a compulsory winding-up order. The total number of cars produced is uncertain, although it is clear that the 1,500 cars per year projection did not materialize. More realistically, volumes were around five cars per week. Registrations of 'new' cars continued into the middle 1960s as batches of components were discovered and built up, and the final production batch of Peerless Phase 2 cars was advertised in June 1964.

LARGE AMERICAN MOTOR IN A LOW-VOLUME LUXURY CAR

At a slight tangent to the Triumph story, a certain Jim Keeble entered the story at this point, with a request to install a large-capacity American V8 engine into a Peerless car, following similar requests from the United States. Keeble eventually joined the company and, latterly with John Gordon, continued the concept of a large American motor in a bespoke British Grand Touring car. It was eventually named the Gordon Keeble, reflecting an earlier attempt in the same market space with a prototype Gordon GT. It was a formula adopted by others, notably AC and Jensen; the latter's Interceptor was perhaps the most commercially successful example of the genre.

ITALIA

The Italia is frequently considered, and not without good reason, to be the most exotic and beautiful of all the cars to have been built on TR underpinnings. Once again using TR3 mechanicals clothed in a new body style, it was conceived at about the same time as the Peerless, and addressed a similar market space. Using the TR3 chassis, engine and transmission, but clothed in coachwork that was classically Italian in style, it is frequently misidentified as a small Ferrari or Maserati – certainly it does not look like an everyday Triumph.

The Idea

The Italia story began towards the end of the 1950s with Doctor Salvatore Ruffino, an Italian entrepreneur who held distribution rights for Standard-Triumph in his home country. Ruffino saw a market for a GT coupé that was a little more 'upmarket' than the TR3, quite likely with an eye on the US market. Starting first with a design by Zagato, which failed to inspire, Ruffino commissioned Giovanni Michelotti to come up with a two-door fixed-head coupé with occasional rear seats. At the same time, Michelotti was developing his relationship with Standard-Triumph and was engaged on the

The most exotic and beautiful TR ever to be built? In the opinion of many, the Italia could be.

Certain design characteristics were shared with Michelotti's TR4 design, notably the bonnet bulge to clear the carburettors and the haunched shoulders just behind the doors. This latter feature was widely used by other designers to convey a sense of power and speed to sports cars.

project to design the replacement for the side-screen cars that became the TR4. It is hardly surprising, therefore, that certain common design features exist between the Michelotti-designed TRs and the Italia.

With a design completed, Ruffino intended to build the cars himself under the auspices of a company called Romanazzi. He learned through the close association between Michelotti and Vignale that the latter had spare capacity that could be utilized to build the new car, allowing it to be introduced to the market in a shorter time scale than would otherwise have been possible. The cars were therefore built at Vignale's facility, but on a line owned by Ruffino. In true bespoke coachbuilding tradition, as employed by Vignale, none of the body panels was formed over a wooden buck, but made to fit each individual car as it was assembled, with the result that no two cars were identical.

Initial testing revealed a small number of issues that required attention, and a front anti-roll bar was subsequently specified, as were seven-leaf rear springs (an additional leaf as compared with the TR3) and higher-rated dampers. All Italias were built with the 1991cc engine. Even at the end of production, when the TR3 rolling chassis had evolved to the TR3B and was normally fitted with the larger engine, the Italias retained the original engine capacity, keeping the car within the important sub-2-litre taxation category prevalent in many countries at the time.

Standard-Triumph productized the sub-assemblies as being specific to the Italia, incorporating the minor suspension modifications and issuing a series of commission numbers in the TS xxxxx CO or TS xxxxx COO range ('CO' signifying 'chassis only' and the additional 'O' designating the fitting of an overdrive unit). The final thirty or so cars that were built on TR3B underpinnings were designated with a 'TSF' prefix. Engines intended to be fitted to the cars were designated with a suffix letter 'I' and were unmodified, other than the addition of a small tab to the rocker cover to hold the capillary tube for the temperature gauge. A locally sourced radiator and heater were fitted, along with many unique electrical and trim fittings, some of which bear similarities with other Italian cars of the period.

Sales and Marketing

Ruffino had initially agreed with Standard-Triumph that each dealer would take one car into stock, making a total of 720 cars. On this basis, plans were set out to produce 500 cars in 1960 and the same number in 1961.

Unfortunately for Dr Ruffino, Standard-Triumph were seriously preoccupied with the rapidly deteriorating financial situation, which was resolved only with the takeover by Leyland Motors. Against the background of the imminent launch of the TR4, interest in the Italia project faded, perhaps because it would provide unnecessary competition for the new Triumph car. The relationship between

Ruffino and Standard-Triumph became embittered. A number of chassis delivered did not meet the agreed specification, and it became clear that Triumph dealers were not going to sell the car, thus denying Ruffino access to the important US market through the Standard-Triumph network.

With the breakdown in relations, Ruffino set out to sell the Italia himself, forming a new business to stand alongside the Triumph set-up. The car became the Italia 2000 and all reference to the Triumph name was lost, except for a badge on the rear wing bearing the inscription 'T M Triumph', now widely accepted to mean *telaio e motore*, or 'chassis and engine'. Distribution in North America was arranged through Stutz Plaisted, a Volvo dealer located in Massachusetts as importer. The Stutz Plaisted business then made arrangements across the country with local dealers.

One significant hindrance to sales was the limited supply of spare parts. Although most of the mechanical items and certainly all the routine servicing requisites were common across the Triumph product range, body parts were a different matter entirely. Customers in Europe could return their cars to Dr Ruffino if bodywork was required, but in the United States owners were obliged to sign a waiver agreement to confirm their understanding that no body parts

The rear wing bore this badge; the letters designated by the flags represent 'Vignale' and 'Standard'.

were available. Bespoke repairs by a skilled body shop were, however, a possibility and, although it was a bureaucratic and logistical challenge, it was feasible to import unique components from Italy.

Production continued until 1962, but, without the support from Triumph and with competition from the lower-priced TR4, the Italia slowly faded away. None the less, several languished in dealerships long after production ended, with at least one car not being registered for the road until the 1980s. Ruffino retained his Triumph distributorship until the mid-1960s. When the agreement was finally terminated, a clause in it required Standard-Triumph to repurchase all his stock and spares, so that the final few Italias still with Ruffino found their way into Triumph's inventory. As they were left-hand-drive cars based on TR3B chassis, they were shipped to the United States, where they eventually found owners; the last few were registered in 1965.

Production never reached the projected 1,000 cars and the records suggest that just 325 chassis were shipped for completion as Italias. Nevertheless, the car is now a highly sought after and consequently valuable TR derivative.

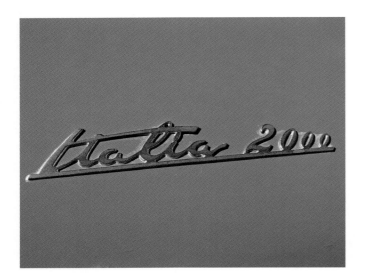

ABOVE LEFT: **The boot lid bore the inscription 'Italia 2000'.**

ABOVE RIGHT: **The cover over the licence-plate holder bore the signature of the designer: 'Styled by G. Michelotti'.**

LEFT: **At the rear of the front wing, just behind the wheel, small Vignale shields were fitted.**

RESCUING AN ITALIA – AN OWNER'S STORY

Paul Harvey, a successful Midlands businessman, has owned TRs since his days as a student and currently owns the green car featured. In 2013, while browsing online, he came across an unusual car being offered for auction that had the appearance of something obviously with Italian origins but with robust British sports-car underpinnings. An online bid of $50,000 failed to meet the reserve price, but his interest had been piqued. Research, including a visit to the Coventry Museum of Transport, confirmed that the car he was looking at was, indeed, the fabled Italia. More investigation led to a classic-car restorer in California and a lead on a green Italia that might be for sale in Italy. Emails followed, pictures were sent. Eventually, an asking price was forthcoming, but it was surely too low for the car to be either original or genuine. A visit to Italy and a physical inspection would be the only way to confirm.

In as-found condition, the car shows very little sign of its age, with just a few cracks in the paintwork. Unusually for an Italian-built car, the paint is a period BMC shade of Almond Green.

continued overleaf

RESCUING AN ITALIA – AN OWNER'S STORY *continued*

The car resided in a dingy back-street garage in a mountain village north of Milan, where Italians have their cars serviced while they are out skiing. The Italia was surrounded by modern vehicles, but revealed itself to be genuine, unrestored and complete. It was first registered in 1981 and had had one single owner, with just over 6,000km (3,700 miles) recorded. A thorough examination showed the car to be complete in all detail; there was some flaking paint, but everything unique to the car was in place, as were the original sales invoice and documents confirming its originality.

A price was agreed with the owner, but a deposit was refused. Rumours reached Paul of interest from a dealer asking about a 'green Italia'; it had to be the same car, so urgent action was called for if the car was not to slip away. Hitching a substantial trailer to his 4x4, Paul decided to drive across Europe to Italy to meet with the garage owner, insisting he would not leave without the car. In true Italian style, a deal was put together over dinner and bank details were supplied so that cash could be deposited.

However, there seemed to be a problem – Paul was warned that there was no chance of crossing the border out of Italy with the car without all the paperwork being in place, and that could take at least two weeks. In the end, the papers were sorted out the following day. The car was loaded on to the trailer and Paul made the journey home to central England. There was just one awkward moment, at the French border exiting the Mont Blanc tunnel. An official stopped the 4x4, commented on the 'nice car', and asked for 'the ticket'. Paul handed over the package of documentation received from the Italian authorities, but was told that all they needed to see was the toll ticket to use the tunnel. There was no need for any paperwork at all. The Triumph chassis number was enough to verify the age of the car, exempting it from VAT on entry to the UK and allowing for the issue of an appropriate registration.

LEFT AND OPPOSITE TOP: **The original interior trim as fitted to this car, looking almost unused. The steering wheel is clearly a Standard-Triumph item and the instruments are similar to those in the TR3. The passenger footrest is unique to the Italia.**

Under the bonnet, everything is completely original. Because the car was not registered until 1981, it was necessary for the additional hoses between the oil filler and air filters to be added, to comply with emissions requirements at the time.

GTR4 DOVE

Although the TR4 introduced the removable metal hard top, the perceived market for a fixed-head coupé based on rugged Triumph mechanicals continued beyond the demise of the side-screen models into the era of the TR4. Jaguar had recently announced their E-Type (or XK-E as it was known in the United States) in both convertible and coupé GT versions and, competing in the same market space as the TR, the Sunbeam Alpine had been converted to a 2+2 coupé by the

The distinctive features of the TR4 are visible in this image of a GTR4 Dove.

long-established coachbuilding firm of Thomas Harrington of Hove, Sussex.

Looking to extend the appeal of their product beyond the Sunbeam, Harringtons conceived a similar treatment for the TR4, the product requirement being the transportation over long distances of a couple and their young children, complete with luggage. It was to provide an ideal solution for the TR owner who might otherwise have been forced to abandon the marque due to parental responsibility. It was hoped that it might also appeal to the older sporting motorist looking for a little more comfort.

At this point, the established Triumph dealer L.F. Dove & Co., based in Wimbledon, south-west London, enters the story as the distribution channel for the Triumph GTR4. The new model was to be positioned slightly closer to the top of the market than the open roadster, so the feeling was that it needed a continental-sounding name. To give a

sense of sophistication, an acute accent was added to 'Dove', resulting in the model name 'Dové'. Officially, it was to be pronounced 'Doh-vey', but the cars were and continue to be known as 'Doves', with the standard English pronunciation. The upmarket image was further developed by incorporating the GT letters into the model name badge fitted to the rear of the car.

Conversion of the car was a simple matter. Complete cars direct from the factory were modified by removal of the boot and rear deck panels. The fuel tank was also removed, to provide a clear space from the rear of the seats through to the rear of the car. A new GRP roof and rear tailgate section was then fitted and trimmed, and new rear quarter windows were installed and trimmed. The rear tail included an opening rear hatch to provide for ease of loading. The roof section was of sufficient height to allow a bench-style rear seat to be fitted, giving around

With the addition of what would now be called a 'hatchback', the Dove provided, in addition to the GT styling, extra luggage capacity and rear seating.

The distinctively stylized 'Dove GTR4' badge was fitted to the rear offside of the car.

32 inches (810mm) of headroom. This was considered to be adequate for two children, up to early teenage years. The increased headroom, coupled with the retention of the original windscreen, gave rise to a somewhat hump-backed side view.

All these modifications required changes in what had been the boot space of the car. The petrol tank was now positioned in the space that had originally been used by the spare wheel; the spare wheel was now located on top of the tank. The new location of the fuel tank and

ABOVE: **The new rear bodywork can be clearly seen. Retaining the original windscreen frame and providing adequate headroom in the rear created a side profile that could be considered to be slightly bulbous.**

LEFT: **With the fuel tank relocated, a new filler was provided and a full-width lifting rear hatch gave access to the luggage space.**

the additional space available for it meant that a long-range fuel tank, a primary requirement for a GT car, could be achieved, with the capacity now increased to 15 gallons (68 litres). Somewhat audaciously, the sales literature made great play of the extra tank size, but conveniently omitted to mention that the additional weight of the car meant that fuel consumption would be increased. As a result, the overall range of the car between fuel stops stayed more or less the same. To cope with the

additional weight, all Doves were treated to a mild tune of the engine.

Overall, the finish of the car gave it the appearance of a factory-built model and not a low-volume conversion. The interior trim was very much to the format of the TR4, but with better-quality materials. Standard-Triumph backed the car with a full warranty, but did not foresee a commercial future for it, deciding against bringing the production in-house and marketing it as a fully fledged TR model. Had they predicted the success of the MGB GT that was to follow a few years later, they may well have taken a different view.

Production was very limited, with around fifty cars being built. The factory records do not differentiate cars dispatched for conversion from cars for sale and the option existed for customers to provide their own cars for conversion. Perhaps the price increment of about 25 per cent over the cost of a TR4 restricted the market, but there was also the issue of Thomas Harrington & Co. being part of the Rootes Brothers empire. Perhaps they had been dissuaded from helping too much in the promotion of a rival manufacturer's product. It is believed that a small number of TR4As were also converted, giving rise to the GTR4A model and at least one later TR 250 has been retrospectively converted in recent years.

ABOVE AND RIGHT: **The interior trim of the Dove conversion was at least as good as that found on an original factory car.**

Designed to address the same market, the Dove GTR4 and later MGB-GT are similar in design. The MG is perhaps more 'flowing', with the increased windscreen height giving more headroom inside the cockpit. This particular MG is the V8 model, another home for the Buick-derived Rover engine also used in the TR7 V8 and TR8.

A TR6 SHOOTING BRAKE?

Although nothing along such lines was offered as a commercial product, a number of owners have found a need for a Grand Touring-oriented TR6 and have undertaken individual conversions. The results were similar to those achieved with the Peerless and Dove, but with TR6 underpinnings.

Below the door line and forward of the B post, the car is a completely standard TR6. The roof was constructed from the panels sourced from a pair of factory hard tops that would otherwise have been scrapped.

The rear three-quarter image shows how the original and modified panels blend together; the rear hatch is again constructed from a factory hard top.

BELOW: **Grinnall cars were finished with a distinctive badge on the bonnet.**

GRINNALL

Most of the cars featured here could be considered to be adaptations of the basic theme of TR on which new body-work was mounted to fill a perceived market need while the TR product range was in volume production. Mark Grinnall's idea was to take a TR7 and develop the car further by adding more power, reworking the suspension and modifying the bodywork to a greater or lesser extent – *after* production by Triumph had ended.

Under the bonnet, the 4-cylinder engine was removed and replaced with the Rover V8 engine, as fitted to the TR8, as a starting point. The owner could then choose to stay with the existing twin SU carburettors or fit a four-barrel Holley carburettor, as widely used on US V8 engines. For the ultimate in power, there was the option of an electronic fuel-injection system. Upgraded brakes were fitted as standard, along with a new five-speed transmission, if required. Finally, wider wheels would usually be added, requiring flared wheel arches.

As the donor cars for the Grinnall conversions could show signs of corrosion, it was normal for the shell to

be stripped to bare metal and any corrosion repaired or replaced. Features such as wheel arches were prefabricated and welded to the body shell, requiring just a minimal skim of filler to complete the transformation and giving a quality factory finish to the rebuilt cars. Additional strengthening was added to minimize scuttle shake and wider section sills completed the transformation.

Grinnall cars could be as subtle or as modified as the owner desired. This example has been fitted with a body kit encompassing wider sills and flared rear wheel arches. It has new wheels and has been repainted in a colour that is even brighter than those offered by the factory in the 1970s.

2+2 'Wedge'

One of the options offered by Grinnall was a 2+2 conversion of the TR7. Removal of the front bulkhead of the boot and a repositioning of the fuel tank allowed a new seat-pan assembly to be fitted, with the boot bulkhead now suitably positioned as part of a rear seat framework. In common with earlier TR conversions to 2+2 format, the space provided was adequate only for children. Athough the loss of boot space restricted the ability to carry luggage, the rear-seat area could be utilized if the seats were not in use.

The Radical Grinnall Mark 2

Nearly forty years after the original design for the TR was conceived, the market still existed for a similar car. With Triumph now consigned to history, the Grinnall company designed an enhanced TR8, possibly following the same route that Triumph may have taken had the manufacturer survived as a stand-alone business.

Taking the earlier Grinnall enhancements as a basis, the Mark 2 car provided a smoother body style and radically increased performance. The body style was modified

LEFT: **Following the earlier themes of rear-seat fittings in TRs, the Grinnall 2+2 conversion provided limited but useable space, probably only really suitable for children.**

BELOW: **The Grinnall Mark 2 design has often been commented on as reflecting what Triumph may have developed as an evolution of the basic TR7 design. The rounding of the edges was very much in keeping with designs of the period, although the basic outline of the original car remained.**

The rear quarter view of the later Grinnall car shows how well the new and the original blend together.

by removing nose and tail sections and replacing them with advanced materials, including GRP, using Kevlar as the reinforcing medium. The side profile of the car was smoothed off, sills extended and wheel arches flared to accommodate the wider-profile wheels and extensive suspension modifications. Steelwork was galvanized to dramatically reduce the risk of corrosion. A minimal amount of filler was then used to blend the old and the new before the completed bodywork was finished in modern paint materials.

Viewed from the front, the car was not dissimilar to its contemporary, the Volvo 480ES; indeed, the front light units had been sourced from the Volvo, although the characteristic pop-up headlights were retained. At the rear, larger lamp clusters, originally designed for the Ford Orion saloon, were fitted. Although the general appearance of the original wedge design remained, the overall feel was of a car that was some twenty years newer. It looked as though it had been designed for the 1990s – which, to all intents and purposes, it had been.

Under the bonnet, the latest in the line of Rover V8 engines was installed, now increased to a capacity of 4.5 litres. The factory demonstrator car illustrated is fitted with a tuned version of this engine developed for the Paris–Dakar rally, producing 275bhp. In order to handle the increased power, the suspension and braking underpinnings were derived from the Rover 3500 SD1 saloon car with Grinnall enhancements, including all-round disc brakes to match the additional power. *Car Mechanics* tested this car in September 1991, concluding that 'the result [was] certainly stylish, but it [was] still rather too broad for its length'. Grinnall's quality was praised, however, as being 'far beyond that of the TR7'.

In total, around 350 Grinnall TR7 and TR8s were built before the business moved on to newer projects. The Grinnall Company remains in business producing specialist high performance three-wheeled motor vehicles.

LEFT: **From the front, again the joins are seamless. The pop-up headlights give away the car's origins; the sidelights and turn signals lamp clusters are as used on the Volvo 480ES.**

BELOW: **Another view of the front, with the headlamp pods raised.**

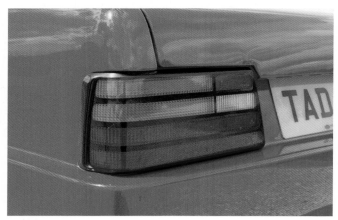

ABOVE: **The rear lamp clusters are the same as used in the Ford Orion.**

Cockpit trim for the Grinnall models followed the established TR7 layout. Wooden dashboards made a reappearance as an option.

The Mark 2 round-bodied Grinnall, perhaps the final iteration of the Triumph TR – unless the current owners of the Triumph marque ever decide to relaunch the model.

STANDARD-TRIUMPH AS A COMPONENT SUPPLIER

While the Triumph company in the 1930s was a customer for specialist suppliers, most notably Coventry-Climax for engines, the Standard Motor Company had established a relationship with other motor manufacturers in the Coventry area to supply substantial components. The most successful arrangement was with SS Cars, soon to become Jaguar, and with Morgan. Subsequently, Standard-Triumph components, particularly engines and suspension, became the products of choice for smaller vehicle constructors.

MORGAN

The introduction of the 4-cylinder wet-liner engine, as fitted in all TRs up until the introduction of the TR5, was of interest to lower-volume manufacturers who were impressed by its power and reliability. Foremost among these was the Morgan Car Company, with whom Sir John Black had a long-standing relationship and which had been a customer for an earlier 1267cc engine. The TR2 engine was supplied to Morgan for the Plus 4 model, but there were concerns over supply-chain security, particularly as the Morgan could be construed as a competitor to the TR range. As a result, Morgan turned to the Ford Motor Company as an alternative supplier for engines to be fitted into its smaller and less powerful cars.

TVR's M series cars dipped into the Triumph component supply, especially the 2500M pictured here, which was essentially the mechanical parts of a US-specification TR6 under a GRP body.

Nevertheless, Morgan did remain as a customer for the 2088cc and 2138cc engines, until production ceased with the ending of TR4A production.

TVR

Introduced in 1972, the TVR M series followed on from the earlier Vixen model and continued the established two-door fixed-head coupé body style constructed from GRP. Three engine types were available: the 1600M and 3000M models were powered by Ford, but the 2500M used the Triumph 2.5-litre engine as fitted to the TR 250 and larger Triumph saloons. The United States was an important marketplace for TVR and this engine came with one key advantage, in that it had already been approved for use in that territory. Triumph also provided the gearbox, differential, steering and front-

suspension components for the car, the same units as those used in the TR6.

TRIDENT CARS LIMITED

Trident Cars was a rather short-lived company based in Suffolk, UK, building sports cars in kit form or as fully built. In 1969, the company introduced their Venturer model, built on a lengthened TR6 chassis but intended to be powered by a Ford 3-litre V6 engine. A new model, the Tycoon, was announced in 1971, now powered by a Triumph 2.5-litre straight-six engine with Lucas petrol injection and the option of automatic transmission. Effectively, the car was a lengthened TR6 with fixed-head coupé bodywork, following in a long tradition of other builders creating similar models from TR underpinnings, starting with the Peerless GT.

An unusually finished Trident Venturer at a 40th anniversary commemorative event. This particular car was an entrant in the 1970 World Cup Rally.

According to data published by the Trident Car Club, it is believed that in total forty-nine Venturers and six Tycoons were produced.

MARCOS MANTIS

Although the model name has subsequently been reused, the original Mantis was a striking if somewhat unusually styled four-seat coupé, built around a space-frame chassis and fitted with a glass-fibre body. The wedge styling of the car predated the general adoption of such designs by several years. Originally, the car was intended to be powered by the Ford 3-litre V6 power plant, but technical difficulties with the transmission led to the Triumph 2.5PI engine in TR tune being fitted. Top speed of 120mph was quoted, along with a 0–60mph time of around eight seconds.

With high performance, comfort and a high-quality trim, the Marcos Mantis was positioned at the top of the market. Its list price was £3,185, some 50 per cent more than the Rover P6B V8-engined 3500, a similar but more conventionally styled car aimed at much the same market. Just thirty-two cars were to be built.

SAAB

Although it was not strictly speaking a TR engine, the basic design of the slant-four engine used in 2-litre form in the TR7 was shipped to SAAB as the power plant to be used in the 99 and subsequent models from 1969 onwards. Hugely successful in rallying, SAAB had originally used two-stroke engines based on a design by DKW before moving to the Ford V4 engine in the 96 family models – perhaps not the most civilized engine for use in a car with aspirations to enter the higher echelons of the market. The SAAB implementation of the Triumph engine had a capacity of 1709cc and produced 88bhp. Reports reached Triumph that SAAB engineers were concerned with manufacturing tolerances and oil consumption, moving on to redesign their own version of a 2-litre engine using the basic Triumph design. Subsequent enhancements to the engine added electronic fuel injection and, ultimately, turbocharging.

INDEX